A SEAT AT THE TABLE FOR WOMEN, GIRLS AND MOVEMENTS

A MANIFESTO ON PEACE AND SECURITY

Abiola Afolayan, Esq.

MG

**MOLO GLOBAL
PUBLISHING**

ISBN Paperback: 978-1-7350720-6-7
ISBN Ebook: 978-1-7350720-9-8
ISBN Hardcover: 978-1-7350720-2-9
Library of Congress Control Number: 2021905160
© Abiola Afolayan, 2021 All Rights Reserved
Published in the United States by Molo Global Publishing, an imprint of Molo Global Consulting, LLC, Maryland.

DEDICATION

This book, my first, is dedicated to my mama Lola, one of the most brilliant women you will ever meet – who through her service to others taught us to always find a way to serve, my late dad Dr. J.L. Afolayan, my siblings and their families, my grandma, Alhaja Nimotallahi-the great storyteller, my friends, all my teachers, mentors, supporters who are too many to name, and my publisher, for believing in this work and pushing me to put in the work to get it to the finish line.

I thank Dr. Kathleen Kuehnast of the United States Institute of Peace (USIP) for her consistent mentorship and feedback throughout the development of this book. I thank my American Bar Association friends and mentors, and especially my colleague Adejoké Babington-Ashaye, former Counsel at the World Bank Group for her peer review of this work. I am also thankful to my friends and mentors at the UN World Food Programme, on Capitol Hill, in the Labor movement and in the Women's movement for their support.

This book is also dedicated to all the women, girls, boys and men across the globe creating a seat at the table towards an equitable world. We are all better off for it.

Very truly yours,

Abiola Afolayan

Late Poet Maya Angelou's poem "Still I Rise" Stanza 3 in French and English
President Barack Obama's statement in "Fact Sheet: Let Girls Learn – A
Comprehensive Investment in Adolescent Girls Education"
First Lady Hillary Rodham Clinton's comments at the United Nations Fourth
World Conference on Women in Beijing

FOREWORD

Making the Invisible Visible: Why We Celebrate These Women

By Dr. Kathleen Kuehnast

This is the 21st Century yet women remain mostly invisible in our global stories. I am an anthropologist working in the realm of women, peace and security, both in the policy and practice arenas, where my team and I analyze different gendered impacts of violence and conflict on both men and women.

In addition, we focus on U.N. Security Council Resolution 1325, including the critical role women should play in all aspects of peacebuilding, especially at the peace table. An equally critical effort is the concept of engaging men and boys in helping to keep peace and security and championing of women's rights.

One of the key tools of our efforts is listening to the stories people tell about themselves. In such stories we begin to understand the human condition.

Stories convey vision and power.

A Seat at the Table reminds us that every time a story is told about a woman or girl, she becomes visible.

Abiola Afolayan challenges us to do just that by showcasing the achievements of women, girls, and movements in propelling the better angels in our world.

Tempered with stories of women from across the globe but from different walks of life, coupled with research and real-life experiences, we see the thread that underlies the accomplishments of the subjects and the author: character, vision, grit, hope, creativity, family and communal support, and male allies.

In many ways, the narratives mirror the life of Abiola who as a Nigerian American has navigated life in multiple continents from Africa to North America to Europe and has been a beneficiary of the actions of the women, girls and movements that she writes about.

I had the honor of listening to Abiola over several years when she first imagined this book. As she sat in my office at the U.S. Institute of Peace, she talked about how she wanted to contribute to the women, peace and security effort. She wanted to illuminate some of the female heroes of her life from across the globe, through storytelling.

Indeed, storytelling is the essence of peacebuilding as it yields hope.

These stories remind us again that most leaders are not born. But instead, such leaders emerge from tough or even inhumane challenges.

The stories help us understand how leaders transform hardship and harsh realities into a new story, something bold to improve the lives of others.

Moreover, these stories help us demystify the human force of resilience and recognize it in the human face of women and girls.

CONTENTS

Part 1

THE RIGHTS AND THE VOTE

Late Chief Mrs. Olufunmilayo Ransome-Kuti of Nigeria, Circa 1960s. Illustration by Sarah Dahir (SOUTH AFRICA)

Late Chief Mrs. Olufunmilayo Ransome-Kuti of Nigeria

Women are central to the safe and prosperous functioning of all societies across the globe. Like the mythical Mulan in the Ballad of Mulan between the fourth and sixth centuries, it is important for women and girls to take their place and allow themselves to be comfortable taking a seat at the table.[1] They should not be made to feel ashamed or hide the true essence of who they are. Indeed, it is in the embracing of one's true essence that one is able to channel who one is made to be. Naturally, this path is often lonely. However, the clarity of being is worth the journey.

On February 18, 1977, close to 1,000 Nigerian military officers attacked activist and musician Fela Kuti's home, Kalakuta Republic, in Lagos, Nigeria, where he and his family resided. His crime: speaking against the Nigerian government's corruption and police brutality upon the protesting populace. His penance: the death of his mother, jail time, seizure of his home, and displacement of his neighbors.[2]

Late Chief Mrs. Olufunmilayo Ransome-Kuti and the first and only Nigerian Prime Minister Sir Abubakar Tafawa Balewa, Circa 1960s

On that fateful Friday, the soldiers burnt down Fela's house, beating him and everybody in the compound. Fela's 77-year old mother, the pioneering activist Chief Mrs. Olufunmilayo Ransome Kuti, was also thrown from a window. She died shortly after from the injuries. The event was dubbed "War on Kalakuta" by Lagosians, Nigerians, and other global sympathizers. Thereafter, Fela made an album entitled "Unknown Soldier" as an ode to his mother, which included the lyrics, "*Dem throw my mama; Out of from window; Dem kill my mama (x5)…*"[3]

Chief Mrs. Olufunmilayo Ransome Kuti also known as the Lioness of Lisabi was indeed an unknown soldier of many social causes in Nigeria.

Aside from being Fela Anikulapo Kuti's mother, she was also the aunt of Africa's first Nobel Laureate, Professor Oluwole Soyinka. What must not be lost was Chief Mrs. Olufunmilayo Ransome Kuti's (Olufunmilayo) standing in Nigerian history.[4] She was fortunate to have attended some of the best schools in Nigeria, providing her the intellectual space to fully develop her personhood, sense of community and the importance of appending her destiny to a cause greater than her.

Olufunmilayo was a fierce human rights advocate, blazing the trail that women's rights are indeed human rights from her work with women and girls of all economic, social and political leaning. She was one of the few women delegates at the table in negotiating Nigerian independence from colonial Britain and she fought for universal suffrage, helping to usher in the rights of women to vote in Nigeria. Olufunmilayo also led a women's economic empowerment movement that ousted a king who sought to unfairly tax Nigerian market women.[5] She fought for the rights of women to be educated and founded a girls' primary school.[6]

The history conveyed to us by the Lioness of Lisabi inspires us to believe that among other classifications, gender, cultural limitations, violence, colonial powers, and police brutality do not have to be stumbling blocks to our self-determination and finding our seat at the table.

The violation of her human right, which led to her death at the hands of Nigerian security forces, underscores the importance of policies and programs that protect women and girls and the faithful enforcement of these measures. The fact that a woman of Olufunmilayo's age and stature in Nigerian society could suffer the brutal attack of Nigerian military forces decades ago, coupled with Nigeria's grappling with violence perpetrated by Nigerian security forces as encapsulated in the #ENDSARS movement,[7] underscores that we have some ways to go in protecting women and girls from violence. It also demonstrates that systemic change, inclusive of a seat and voice at the table is what will lead to effective change towards the protection of human rights for women and girls in all contexts.

United Nations Universal Declaration of Human Rights (UNUDHR)

According to Article 1 of the United Nations Universal Declaration of Human Rights, "all human beings are born free and equal in dignity and rights." Article 2 adds that everyone "is entitled to all the rights and freedoms set forth in this Declaration, without distinction of any kind, such as race, colour, sex, language, religion, political or other opinion, national or social origin, property, birth or other status. Furthermore, no distinction shall be made on the basis of the political, jurisdictional or international status of the country or territory to which a person belongs, whether it be independent, trust, non-self-governing or under any other limitation of sovereignty."[8] In essence, the global community, through this declaration, has agreed to uphold these universal values at home and in comity with one another. In exchange, the world should enjoy peace, security, and economic prosperity. Where any human right is infringed upon, we find unrest, instability, violence against the underrepresented members of such a society, and social and political regression. This is why upholding rights is essential, especially for women and girls, in light of the global history of their being viewed as inferior, even though they are central to the health of any and every community. From an economic perspective, investment in initiatives that uphold the rights of women and girls is good for social and political structures. Also, equity and equality reflect the better angels[9] in all of us and showcases humanity's best. Internationally, some women had a seat at the table during the drafting of the UNUDHR.

Indeed, in 1946, late U.S. First Lady Eleanor Roosevelt was appointed as a delegate to the United Nations General Assembly by late President Harry S. Truman. She was posthumously awarded the Human Rights Prize for her work on the inclusion of women's rights in the Universal Declaration-editing the phrase "All men are born free and equal" to "All human beings are born free and equal" in Article 1 of the Universal Declaration of Human Rights.[10] Although Lady Roosevelt clearly had a seat at the table as Chairperson of the Commission on Human Rights and the drafting of the Universal Declaration of Human Rights, the rights of women domestically in the U.S. was slow moving, notwithstanding the ratification of the 19th Amendment to the U.S. Constitution.

19ᵗʰ Amendment to the U.S. Constitution

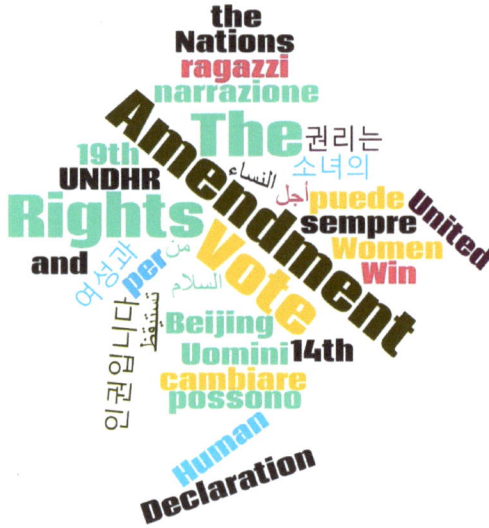

Various languages on the importance of civic engagement

On or about August 26, 1920, three-quarters of the United States state legislatures ratified the 19ᵗʰ Amendment to the U.S. Constitution, granting American women the right to vote, upon the signing of a proclamation by U.S. Secretary of State Bainbridge Colby.[11] However, does progress, a seat at the table and human rights towards gender equality really start with the right to vote? Dr. Kathleen Kuehnast, Director of Gender Policy and Strategy at the U.S. Institute of Peace and Dr. Nora Dudwick, Director, Gender and Social Inclusion at the Millennium Challenge Corporation, both cultural anthropologists, argue that the golden hour for gender is not after the peace treaties have been signed but before the signatures take place. They posit that the social contract on gender equality must be conceived before the crisis has ended, then written into the new Constitution, implemented in the reconfigured institutions, and prioritized in newly developed education textbooks.[12] But what happens if there are no women like Chief Mrs. Olufunmilayo Ransome Kuti and First Lady Eleanor Roosevelt present in the "golden hour"? I like to call this the nexus for gender empowerment, equality, and equity – policy measures-institutional measures-educational measures – which help frame the discussion throughout this manifesto. Whether in crisis and or in peace, when we are in good health or ill, when a new Constitution is being drafted or when the world faces a world war, climate disaster, or a global pandemic such as COVID 19, which poses an existential threat to our peace and security, women and girls at the table amid the crisis is imperative. This should go without saying, but we must sometimes state the obvious for our political and social will to be catalysed.

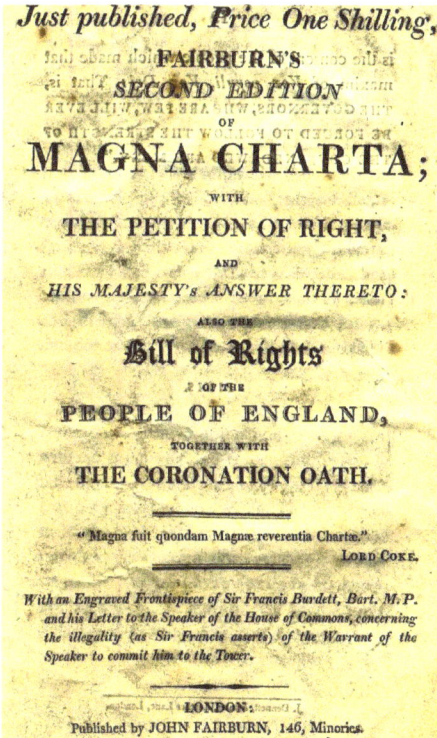

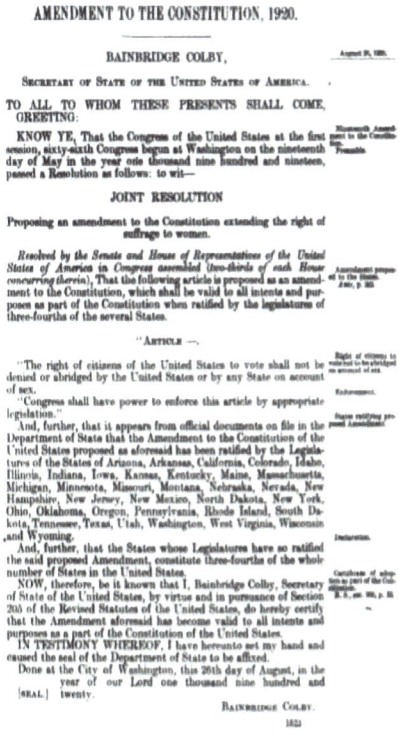

In addition to the Declaration of Independence, the U.S. Constitution is one of the United States' key founding documents. It includes the Bill of Rights, which lists many rights to protect everyone, many of which draw inspiration from the Magna Carter. The Magna Carta was drafted to curtail the tyrannical monarch, King John.[13]

The U.S. Constitution declares that we are all created equal, regardless of what we look like, who we are friends with or what we believe. For example, the First Amendment protects everyone's right to free speech, freedom to assemble, and the freedom to have a religion or no religion. However, undergirding the enforcement of rights, whether in the 19th or First Amendment, is the equal protection articulated in the 14th Amendment to the U.S. Constitution, which protects the civil liberties articulated in the Bill of Rights of the United States Constitution. Observing the protections, the historical documents suggest an awareness of the inequity that existed in society - here particularly the injustice of slavery and the importance of combatting these inequities through policy by the framers of the U.S. Constitution.

14th Amendment to the U.S. Constitution

On or about July 9, 1868, the 14th Amendment to the United States Constitution was ratified. As one of the Reconstruction era amendments, it granted citizenship to all persons born or naturalized in the United States—including former slaves—and guaranteed all citizens "equal protection of the laws."[14] Indeed, the shameful act of slavery triggered the civil war in the U.S., making it important to create a seat at the table for African Americans[15] where there were irreconcilable differences between the free and slave states over the prohibition of slavery.[16]

Over 152 years later, the 14th Amendment ensures we are equally protected before the law to exercise all of our rights, regardless of what we look like, who are our friends or what we believe. In other words, the U.S. Constitution is supposed to be color, sex and status blind. However, racial injustices, too numerous to name reflect a need for continued reckoning with the fairness of enforcing the Constitution.[17]

Notwithstanding the protections articulated in the 14th Amendment, women in the United States, who were judged on the basis of sex, were not granted the right to vote until much later, in 1920, vis-a-vis the 19th Amendment[18] which gave women the right to vote into office whomever they wanted to represent them in government. One could argue that women in the U.S. missed the "golden hour" because they were not at the table during the drafting of the U.S.' founding documents and policies, erecting key institutions, or the formulation of education policies. One could also deduce that because of their explicit absence, through no fault of their own, these women and their allies vowed that "never again" would they allow their voices to be silenced during future "golden hour" opportunities. We saw this underscored in the organizing and mobilization that anchored and buoyed the analysis and rationale behind the Equal Rights Amendment in the United States and other global efforts in the movement towards women's empowerment.[19]

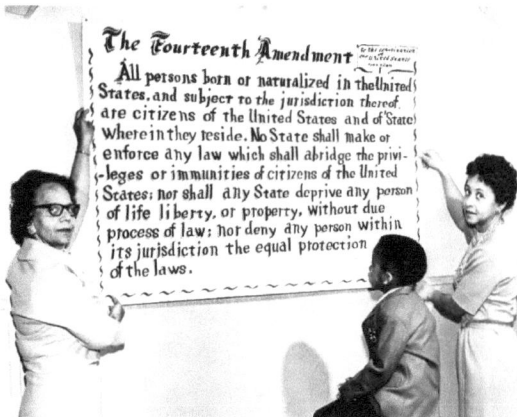

Nigeria and Elsewhere

Globally, the movement towards the rights of women continues to evolve. Earlier on, in the 19th and 20th centuries, women were exercising their right to self-determination through the suffragist efforts. That is, the right to be viewed and treated equally before the law.

For example, in Nigeria, one of the most populous countries in Africa, women advocated for and earned the right to vote in 1979 in the Northern region, and 1954 in the other regions. In Nigeria, the right to vote was viewed as a property right as opposed to a political right. Indeed, the ground work was laid by women like Chief Mrs. Olufunmilayo Ransome Kuti, an African suffragist, who was a key leader of the Egba women in Abeokuta, Ogun State, during a campaign against the arbitrary taxation of women, leading to the abdication of the high king Oba Ademola II in 1949.[20] Born in Abeokuta, Nigeria, she was one of the first female students to attend and integrate the Abeokuta Grammar School and the first woman to drive in the Western Region of Nigeria.[21] The right to drive, emblematic of the freedom of movement enshrined in Article 13 of the Universal Declaration of Human Rights, is one some may take for granted. It should be noted that this right was not granted to women in Saudi Arabia until 2018.[22]

Olufunmilayo spearheaded the creation of the Nigerian Women's Union and the Federation of Nigerian Women's Societies, advocated for Nigerian women's right to vote, and became a noted member of international peace and women's rights movements. At a time of hyper patriarchy, women pursuing a seat at the political table were considered "promiscuous" and "shameless." Yet, she was a prolific figure in Nigerian politics. For example, in the 1950s, she was granted an Oloye Chieftaincy title in Yoruba, an honor typically given to men.[23] A first in many traditional male roles, she was the first woman appointed to the Western House of Chiefs.[24] Additionally, her activism and global speaking engagements spoke truth to power from an African woman's perspective, reminiscent of Nigerian writer Chimamanda Ngozi Adichie.[25] Indeed, Olufunmilayo caused a stir after she penned an article for the *Daily Worker* that argued British colonialism had "severely marginalized" Nigerian women both politically and economically.[26]

Underscoring this trend of property rights and economic rights being tied to political rights is the fact that women who owned property gained the right to vote in the Isle of Man in Europe in 1881. Additionally, theirs was one of the first national parliaments to give women the vote in a general election.[27]

India, one of the most populous nations in Asia, granted women full voting rights in 1949, a couple of years after India's independence from the United Kingdom.[28] Given that women's right to vote was just beginning to gain momentum at this point in history, these achievements were quite revolutionary. These womenfolk were at the frontiers of the women's movement in their respective quarters, while also building a stronghold for the global movement. However, on a day-to-day basis, women were still faced with discrimination, struggling for equality and self-determination, and opportunity for development across the globe.

That women's rights are tied to human rights and opportunity for development is highlighted in the Convention on the Elimination of Discrimination Against Women (CEDAW), an international treaty described as an international bill of rights for women. Adopted in 1979, CEDAW consists of a preamble and 30 articles defining what constitutes discrimination against women and sets an agenda for national action to end such discrimination.[29]

The Convention defines discrimination against women as "...any distinction, exclusion or restriction made on the basis of sex which has the effect or purpose of impairing or nullifying the recognition, enjoyment or exercise by women, irrespective of their marital status, on a basis of equality of men and women, of human rights and fundamental freedoms in the political, economic, social, cultural, civil or any other field."[30] As parties to the Convention, nations commit themselves to undertake a series of measures to end discrimination against women in all forms. Other relevant provisions provide that the basis for realizing equality between women and men is through ensuring women's equal access to, and equal opportunities in, political and public life, including the right to vote and to stand for election, as well as education, health, employment and protection from violent words and actions.

Expressly, member states party to the CEDAW agree to take all appropriate measures, including legislation and temporary special measures, to ensure that women can enjoy all their human rights and fundamental freedoms, all of which are tied to their self-determination. In essence, the right to self-determination is the right of a people to determine their own destiny. In particular, the principle allows people to choose their own political status and decide their own form of economic, cultural, and social development.[31]

National and international measures, and the achievements of the women show us that it takes people and policies to make a change in peace and security, and rewrite the boundaries that are actual or perceived.

Belfast, Northern Ireland. 8 Mar 2014 - Signs are held which say "Implement UNSCR 1325 Now" at International Women's Day.
Credit: Stephen Barnes

History shows us that having women at the table has yielded seminal policy measures that continue to catalyze change and uphold human rights. For example, in addition to the 19th Amendment to the U.S. Constitution, a non-exhaustive list of seminal measures championed by women and their allies include: 1) The UN Security Council Resolution 1325 on Women, Peace and Security - particularly relevant given that the world is currently fraught with violence against women and girls, which is an existential threat to all of their rights as it relates to education, economic empowerment, health, and the climate. 2) The UN Security Council Resolution 1820, which deems rape and acts of sexual violence in the context of armed conflict as a war crime, a crime against humanity, or a constitutive act akin to genocide. It obligates member states to prosecute persons responsible for such actions. 3) The UN Security Council Resolution 1794, which addresses country-specific violence against women and the girl child. It acknowledges the intersection of violence and culture being endemic in different parts of the world and addresses the taboo of discussing these issues. Ultimately, societies that are violent towards women and girls undermine the achievement of equality, development, and peace. 4) The UN Convention on the Rights of the Child (CRC), which provides that children are not just objects who belong to their parents and for whom decisions are made, nor are they adults in training. Instead, children are human beings and individuals with their own rights. The CRC recognizes that childhood is separate from adulthood and is a special, protected time in which children must be allowed to grow, learn, play, develop and flourish with dignity. 5) The Paris Agreement, an implementing agreement for the United Nations Framework Convention on Climate Change (UNFCCC), which deals with proactively addressing greenhouse gas emissions, needed mitigation measures, and finances to achieve the climate change objectives that work to ensure that countries where women and girls predominate and are typically in the eye of the storm are not obliterated as a result of climate inertia. 6) The Fourth World Conference on Women and the adoption of the Beijing Declaration and Platform for Action (1995), which seeks to accelerate the realization of gender equality and women and girls' empowerment everywhere.

When women and girls win, the world wins on all fronts. Although the cumulative efforts of the collective toil and labor may at first seem to be in vain, we must take heart that like a mustard seed, with more women and girls at the table, women's struggle towards equal rights, equity, respect of her vote and protection from all forms of violence will bear a powerful, resilient and effective fruit for all humankind.

TWELVE REASONS

WHY WOMEN SHOULD VOTE

1. **BECAUSE** it is the foundation of all political liberty that those who obey the Law should have a voice in choosing those who make the Law.

2. **BECAUSE** most Laws affect women as much as men, and some Laws affect women more than they do men.

3. **BECAUSE** the Laws which affect women are now passed without consulting them.

4. **BECAUSE** Laws affecting children should be regarded from the woman's point of view as well as the man's.

5. **BECAUSE** questions affecting the home come up for consideration in every session of the Legislature and of Congress.

6. **BECAUSE** women have experience which should be helpfully brought to bear on legislation.

7. **BECAUSE** to deprive women of the vote is to lower their position in common estimation.

8. **BECAUSE** the possession of the vote would increase the sense of responsibility among women toward questions of public importance.

9. **BECAUSE** public-spirited mothers mean public-spirited sons.

10. **BECAUSE** large numbers of intelligent, thoughtful, hard-working women desire the franchise.

11. **BECAUSE** the objections raised against their having the franchise are based on sentiment, not on reason.

12. **BECAUSE** to sum up all reasons in one—IT IS FOR THE COMMON GOOD OF ALL.

WOMEN SUFFRAGE PARTY

27 Lafayette Avenue   Brooklyn, N. Y.

Part 2

WOMEN, GIRLS, PEACE AND SECURITY

Late Supreme Court Justice Ruth Bader Ginsburg and I in Washington, DC at the American Bar Association (ABA) Rule of Law Initiative event honoring her with its 2016 ABA Rule of Law Award for her commitment to the global advancement of the rule of law, Illustration by Sarah Dahir (SOUTH AFRICA)

United Nations Security Council Resolution 1325 on Women Peace and Security

The first all-female unit of United Nations peacekeepers stand at attention as they arrive at Roberts International Airport outside Liberia's capital Monrovia January 30, 2007. The group of more than 100 police women from India will stay in Liberia for six months, helping to train the local police force. REUTERS/ Christopher Herwig (LIBERIA)

Adopted in October 2000, the United Nations Security Council Resolution 1325 (UNSCR 1325) is a seminal international measure that advances gender equality. According to international law scholars, 1325 seeks to rewrite the role and seats women are apportioned within the context of war and peace. Resolution 1325 was one of the first formal and legal documents from the Security Council that required parties in a conflict to prevent violations of women's rights, to support women's participation in peace negotiations and post-conflict reconstruction, and to protect women and girls from sexual and gender-based violence in armed conflict.[32] It "urges member states to ensure increased representation of women at all decision-making levels [as it relates to maintaining peace and security] in national, regional and international institutions and [puts in place] mechanisms for the prevention, management, and resolution of conflict."[33]

Now imagine for a minute a world without women's right to vote, from which emanates other rights such those espoused in UNSCR 1325. Without women's right to vote, would we have had a Ruth Bader Ginsburg to advocate for and inspire us around the Equal Rights Amendment and uphold the rule of law in the United States' highest court? Would we have had a Condoleezza Rice serving in the highest foreign policy office of the United States as Secretary of State and National Security Advisor? What about Zozibini Tunzi, a 26-year South African woman crowned Ms. World, not only for her beauty but also for her message and platform on women's empowerment and ending violence against women and girls? Would there be a Malala Yousafzai, a Pakistani youth activist who was so keenly aware of the universal and inalienable right to education for her and her friends to inspire us, propelling the creation of the "Let Girls Learn Initiative" in the United States? And let us not forget the clarion call of "How dare you?"[34] and the righteous defiance of Greta Thunberg on the importance of protecting the environment so that we all do not go extinct. In solidarity with all of the brave women who have been speaking truth to justice about the sexual assault they have suffered, the TIME'S UP movement exists to provide legal representation to survivors as they reclaim their livelihoods and exercise their unalienable right to the safety and security of their bodies.

Through the Black Lives Matter Movement, created by Black women, the world was awakened to the reality of violence upon persons of color globally. The grit and efforts of these women and girls are literally and symbolically embodied in many women and girl leaders, including Kamala Harris-the first woman vice president of the United States. We have seen women activists helping to push for change in Tahrir Square and during the Liberian Civil war. The common thread is that whether they are in the courts, classrooms, in the UN suites, in the oval office or the market streets, when women take their place and lend their talent and their voices, they redefine the status quo and make a change to the benefit of all of society. Interestingly, some of the efforts by women to mobilize their neighbors towards positive change have been construed as angry and violent, reflecting the antiquated misappropriation and mischaracterization of women's efforts – a form of dog-whistle utilized as a violent and cancel culture tactic to scare and silence women who speak out.

The fact is that violent policies, intentions, words, and actions threaten the peace, security and stability of the community as a whole when directed towards women and girls. Thus, regardless of their political affiliation, these women bring to bear the spirit and intent of UNSCR 1325 and, more importantly, underscore that equality and access to peace, security, and economic empowerment are non-partisan issues. Hopefully, more women, girls, and movements will continue to enable the realization of 1325 and other international and local measures committed to the empowerment of women and girls. This realization is essential for resilient change. The elements of 1325 are as follows: the creation and facilitation of inclusive legal frameworks; recruiting women and girls as part of strategic groups working to counter violent extremism; appointing women as leaders in peace processes; increasing women and girls' political leadership; meeting the needs of displaced women and girls; empowering women in the military; providing the platform for more women with disabilities;

preventing violent words and actions against women; engaging male allies; and combatting the issue of women and girls exploited through human trafficking.

As of Fall 2020, the United States, plus 85 countries, created National Action Plans (NAPs) to activate 1325 in their respective countries.[35] The NAP in the United States was catalyzed by President Obama's Executive Order (EO) 13595, which in relevant part acknowledges the importance of 1325 in advancing peace, national security, economic, social development, and international cooperation. EO 13595 asserts that it shall be the policy and practice of the United States Executive Branch to have a National Action Plan on women peace and security. Indeed, the U.S. NAP is a national integration and institutionalization of a gender-responsive approach to diplomatic, development, and defense-related work in conflict contexts.[36] Additionally, the U.S. Congress passed the Women, Peace, and Security Act, which was subsequently signed into law. The Act underscores the dividends of creating opportunities for women and girls to serve as agents of peace via political, economic, and social empowerment. Most recently, in 2019, as part of the whole of government requirements prescribed by the Act, the United States also promulgated its Strategy on Women, Peace, and Security (WPS).

Is it enough that there are measures on the books? Or do we need brave women, girls, and movements to breathe life into the words on paper? How does one make a change in peace and security and rewrite boundaries by implementing 1325 and other gender empowerment measures, given the challenging issues of disease, conflict, and climate crises? What is in the DNA of the remarkable women in this manifesto that gives them such resilient commitment to their work? Is there a thread that each of them shares that provide us further insights and inspire us towards the change we wish to see? How did these women and girls operate individually and collectively within a movement without losing view of the "big picture" of the interconnectedness of their actions in catalyzing global change? Are there causal factors that shape the incidents, dynamics, challenges, and achievements of peace and security initiatives for women and girls in the global order? Is truth indeed like a lion? Need we not defend it? Is it enough to let it loose? Can it defend itself?[37]

Equal Rights and Inferiority: Late U.S. Supreme Court Justice Ruth Bader Ginsburg (RBG)

Speaker of the United States House of Representatives Nancy Pelosi (Democrat of California), alongside several House Democrats and advocates for the amendment, delivers remarks during a news conference on removing the deadline for ratifying the Equal Rights Amendment at the United States Capitol in Washington, DC, U.S. on Wednesday, February 12, 2020. Credit: Stefani Reynolds/CNP

On August 10, 1993, Ruth Bader Ginsburg (RBG), upon nomination by President Bill Clinton and confirmation by the U.S. Senate, took her seat on the bench of the United States Supreme Court.[38] RBG's story inspires us that gender, laws, and the time we are born and placed in history do not have to be a stumbling block to making an indelible mark in the world.

President Jimmy Carter meets with Ruth Bader Ginsburg in The Oval Office after he appointed her to the U.S. Court of Appeals for the District of Columbia Circuit, where she served until her appointment to the Supreme Court in 1993
Contributor: American Photo Archive

RBG, on whose shoulders many efforts around women's equality in the United States stands, embodies the spirit of change and fierceness needed to procure peace and security for women and girls. Her body of work provides contemporary historical backdrop of the work surrounding women's rights in the U.S., especially amid the continuous exclusion of women in various spheres of society, notwithstanding the ratification of the 19th Amendment and the transmission of the Equal Rights Amendment (ERA) to the states for ratification.

Building on the suffragists efforts, culminated, RBG's body of work helped lay additional framework and foundation for future women's rights advocacy in the United States. She drew public awareness to the U.S. Constitution, specifically the Fifth Amendment's Due Process Clause and the 14th Amendment's Equal Protection Clause, as requiring heightened Constitutional scrutiny in matters related to women's rights in U.S. Courts.

Her intellectual mobilization efforts catalyzed discourse on gender equality and what it means practically- for example, through her work on the American Civil Liberty Union's (ACLU) impact litigation campaign for gender equality.

Many of the gender equity cases litigated in the 70s are part of RBG's body of work, some of which she argued before the Supreme Court, prior to her appointment to the Supreme Court. Appointed after Supreme Court Justice Sandra Day O'Connor, RBG made history as the second woman appointed to the U.S. Supreme Court. RBG remained one of three female justices on the Supreme Court, serving along with President Obama appointees: Justice Sonia Sotomayor, the first Latino and Puerto Rican American, and Justice Elena Kagan, of Jewish descent, until her death in September 2020.

Get Your Knee Off of My Neck

Being denied the opportunity to apply one's talent is the equivalent of a suffocating knee on one's neck. In the Fall of 1973, RBG authored an article in the American Bar Association (ABA) Journal entitled: "The Need for the Equal Rights Amendment." At that time in her career, RBG was the first tenured woman law professor at Columbia University, was coordinator of the American Civil Liberties Union Women's Rights Project, and a member of the Board of Editors of the ABA Journal.[39]

Indeed, 1973 was over 50 years after the ratification of the 19th Amendment, and a time when proponents of the Equal Rights Amendment (ERA) had finally prevailed in getting the ERA passed in Congress after numerous efforts by the National Women's Party, who continued to introduce the ERA consistently after the passage of the 19th Amendment. The Suffragist Movement understood that the 19th Amendment did not fix the language in the Constitution that referred to men without reference to women, hence the conclusion that only a separate amendment vis-a-vis the ERA could address this issue.[40] Notably, a similar effort was led by First Lady Eleanor Roosevelt in 1946 during the drafting of the UN Universal Declaration of Human Rights.[41]

In her ABA Journal article, RBG analyzed how mid-nineteenth century feminists looked to Congress after the American Civil War for an express guarantee of equal rights for men and women, primarily because the text of the 14th Amendment raised concerns as it relates to a sex equality guarantee. The main consternation centered on the second section of the 14th Amendment, which placed the word "male" in the Constitution. It featured the word three times, successively, and always in tandem with the term "citizen," so that the grand phrases of the first section of the 14th Amendment, the Due Process and Equal Protection of the Law clauses, would have a qualified – not guaranteed – application to women since women were not explicitly mentioned.

RBG articulated that the concerns were well placed because "the notion that men and women stand as equals before the law was not the original understanding of the Congress that framed the Civil War amendments. Thomas Jefferson put it this way: "Were our state a pure democracy there would still be excluded from our deliberations women, who, to prevent deprivation of morals and ambiguity of issues, should not mix promiscuously with the gatherings of men."[42]

RBG cites the prevailing frame of mind at the time she wrote her article in various instances. For example, a candid response from the Air Force Academy Superintendent: "We will enroll women in 1975 if the amendment [ERA] is ratified. If the amendment is not ratified, women will have to wait a long time before they can expect to enroll."[43] Other examples of the prevailing frame of mind in the country included an Arizona law which stipulated that the Governor, Secretary of State, and Treasurer must be male, a law in Ohio that stated only men may serve as arbitrators in county court proceedings, and in Wisconsin, barbers were licensed to cut men's and women's hair, but cosmeticians could attend to women only.[44]

The ERA raises concern around the use of the word "men" to be synonymous with "citizens" in the U.S. Constitution. It seeks to clarify that "[e]quality of rights under the law shall not be denied or abridged by the United States or by any State on account of sex. The Congress shall have the power to enforce, by appropriate legislation, the provisions of this article. This amendment shall take effect two years after the date of ratification."[45]

RBG argued in the 1970s that the ERA looks toward a legal system in which each person will be judged on individual merit and not on the basis of an unalterable trait of birth that has no necessary relationship to ability. This was in contravention with Jefferson's assertion of a "pure democracy requiring the exclusion of women to prevent promiscuity"[46] since sex is indeed an unalterable trait at birth.

Like the 19th Amendment, the arguments against the ERA have been similar and based on widely debunked theories. These include, but are not limited to, assertions that the sexes mixing could trigger promiscuity, that women are simply intellectually inferior, that women may be required to serve in the military, for which they are ill equipped, and that women lack the physical and intellectual abilities to carry out various professions, such as lawyering and bartending.

In addition to RBG being "Exhibit A" of a woman's ability, with accolades that include graduating first in her law school class, there are additional voices that provide empirical evidence of what women offer when granted their due course at the table. According to General Dwight D. Eisenhower, "…like most old soldiers, I was violently against women soldiers. I thought a tremendous number of difficulties would occur, not only of an administrative nature but others of a more personal type that would get us into trouble. None of that occurred. In the disciplinary field, they were a model for the Army. More than this, their influence throughout the whole command was good. I am convinced that in another war, they have got to be drafted just like the men."[47]

Moreover, according to RBG, citing the Federal Legislation Committee of the Association of the Bar of the City of New York, "[t]he Amendment would eliminate patent discrimination, including all laws which prohibit or discourage women from making full use of their political and economic capabilities on the strength of notions about the proper "role" for women in society."[48]

Adds RBG, "the equal rights amendment, in sum, would dedicate the nation to a new view of the rights and responsibilities of men and women.

It firmly rejects sharp legislative lines between the sexes as constitutionally tolerable. Instead, it looks toward a legal system in which each person will be judged on the basis of individual merit and not on the basis of an unalterable trait of birth,"[49] here, sex.

The Money Maker and Equal Pay

This manifesto is anchored by suffragists across the globe, trailblazers like RBG, women like Belva Lockwood, the first woman ever to gain admission to the U.S. Supreme Court Bar in 1879 and the first woman to appear on official ballots for U.S. presidency in 1884 and 1888.[50] Indeed, across racial lines, women were doing great things and setting the bar. For example, Madam C.J. Walker, was an African-American woman born into freedom, but still with limited-to-no access to education and opportunity. Nevertheless, she became a haircare entrepreneur, philanthropist, political and social activist. As an advocate of black women's independence, Madam Walker created jobs and economic opportunities for thousands of African-American women and was recorded as the first female self-made millionaire in America in the Guinness Book of World Records.[51] Without these predecessors, who surmounted so much adversity, would today's women, girls, and movements have the opportunity to flourish?

It is precisely because of the grit and passion of these predecessors that villages, communities, and nations must continue to train girls to develop their voices, aspire to greatness, solve social policy issues, speak truth to justice unapologetically, and empower others.

In spite of, and perhaps because she was a survivor of sex discrimination throughout her law school and legal career, notwithstanding her superior academic and physical stamina, RBG chose the path of working to chip at changing the narrative and working to gain seats for women at the table, even as she served on the Supreme Court bench.

For example, upon commencing her judicial role, RBG continued to uphold women's rights through her rulings, dissenting, and concurring opinions, making Lady Justice so proud. An illustration is her ruling as the lead author of the Court's opinion in the Virginia Military Institute (VMI) case.[52] The Court held that VMI's denial of admission to women violated the 14th Amendment's Equal Protection Clause, a revolutionary U.S. Constitutional principle as applied to gender equality in that time in history.

Furthermore, her dissent in the Ledbetter case[53] helped to galvanize public attention and catalyze legislative change related to equal pay. In that case, Ledbetter, a female employee of Goodyear Tire, the only woman employed as an Area Manager in 1997 found out that there existed a 15% to 40% disparity between her salary and her fifteen male counterparts. Although a federal jury found that Ledbetter received unequal pay, more likely than not because of her sex, the Supreme Court nullified the verdict, holding that Ledbetter filed her claim too late. In her dissenting opinion, RBG wrote, "[t]he ball is in Congress' court to correct the Court's parsimonious reading of Title VII (U.S. principal law prohibiting employment discrimination)." Following RBG's dissent, the U.S. Congress responded within days with legislative measures introduced in both chambers of Congress to amend Title VII and make it clear that each pay-check that a woman in Ledbetter's situation received renewed the discrimination. The case also clarified that each such pay-check restarted the clock within which a suit could be brought. Subsequently, Congress passed the Lilly Ledbetter Fair Pay Act, one of the first corrective measures President Obama signed into law after taking office. Imagine if we had no RBG on the bench, at the table, or during discussions on the Ledbetter matter, challenging other branches of government to do the right thing? Would we have a Ledbetter Fair Pay Act?

Even with the Ledbetter Fair Pay Act, and other efforts globally, according to the World Bank Group's (WBG) Women Business and the Law reports, with research covering 190 economies from 1971 to 2020, there is a substantial nexus between inequality of opportunity for women and labor market dynamics. According to the reports, women's employment and entrepreneurship are affected by legalized gender discrimination, which adversely affects women and girls' economic outcomes.[54]

What we learn from cases like Ledbetter, and policy research from organizations such as the WBG, is that more measures must continue to be implemented to ensure women's equality. We also learn that the journey of getting women and girls to the table and in achieving parity is not a straight one, but one which ebbs and flows. Nonetheless, it must be pursued vigorously and requires vigilance to ensure protection from one generation to the other. Change is sustainable when generations draw strength from one another and from villages and communities of support.

RBG highlighted her belief that women and girls, like men and boys, need their supporters and mentors to soar. For example, in many speeches, she has mentioned that her inner strength came from various persons around her. Chief among them was her mother, Celia, who herself was a high achieving student who graduated high school early at the age of fifteen with top grades. However, she could not attend college in the early 1920s because higher education and social advancement were reserved for the boy child and not the girl child.

Deprived of the opportunity to further her education, Celia had a heightened understanding that education for a young woman gave her a pathway to self-determination, and thus encouraged her daughter Ruth to excel at everything she did. She did this even as she battled cancer, to which she lost her life a day before Ruth graduated high school with admission to Cornell University. Another indelible mark upon RBG was her aunt, who exposed her to the arts at the Brooklyn Academy of Music. When RBG was 11 years old, she viewed a condensed version of La Gioconda, a production designed for children's imagination and appreciation for opera. This catapulted RBG's love for opera and ignited her fantasy to become a great diva, underscoring art's importance in stimulating the mind, intellect, and imagination. It is her love for the arts, and opera in particular, that would nurture her close friendship with one of her Supreme Court colleagues with whom she always disagreed on the bench, the late Justice Antonin Scalia. Finally, and unequivocally, RBG's late husband, Marty Ginsburg, a tax lawyer, was a powerful force in her life on a professional and personal level. He always served as her number one cheerleader, including carrying the ball forward to make sure her Supreme Court judgeship nomination came to fruition.

RBG and I

I met Justice Ruth Bader Ginsburg in the Fall of 2016 at an American Bar Association Rule of Law Initiative (ABA-ROLI) program in Washington, DC. This was also a culmination and celebration of different roles, where I had the opportunity to serve, including as an African Council Member for the ABA-ROLI. That evening, RBG made a mark on me. She gave a talk on the importance of the rule of law for our society. But her eloquence and inspiring words aside, what struck me most about her was her ability to see everyone in her audience. Perhaps this was because throughout her life, because she is a woman, she had often been overlooked and not seen. RBG's intentional way of being underscores why she is an anchor for change and will remain in the annals of history as a trailblazer for women and girls the world over, while engaging and challenging male allies.

Diplomacy and Violence: U.S. Former Secretary of State and National Security Advisor Dr. Condoleezza Rice

Mourning family of one of the four African American girls killed in the 16th Street Baptist Church bombing on September 15, 1963
Contributor: Everett Collection Historical

On Sunday, September 15, 1963, a bomb exploded during morning services at the 16th Street Baptist Church in Birmingham, Alabama, killing four young girls.

The girls were: Addie Mae Collins, Cynthia Wesley, Carole Robertson, and Carol Denise McNair. The church bombing was the third in Birmingham in 11 days by the Ku Klux Klan (KKK) in defiance of a federal order to integrate Alabama's school system as part of civil rights efforts to facilitate equal protection under the law for African-Americans. 15 sticks of dynamite were planted in the church basement, underneath what turned out to be the girls' restroom.[55] The attack rocked the sense of security of girls, women, and the community as a whole.

What role can women foreign ministers play in making the world safer for women and girls in war and in peace?

42 years later, on January 26, 2005, upon nomination by President George W. Bush and confirmation by the U.S. Senate, Dr. Condoleezza Rice took a seat at the table and commenced her position as the first African-American woman to serve as Secretary of State.[56]

Rice's friend, 11-year-old Denise McNair, was one of the girls who died in the church bombing in her hometown of Birmingham, Alabama.[57]

Rice's story inspires us to believe, as we observed in awe her rewriting the boundary of what a Secretary of State could look like on many dimensions.[58] For this manifesto, my analysis of Rice's trajectory hinges, like in RBG's case, on an assessment of the life experiences that contributed to who she is and how she negotiates life.

No More Rape as a Weapon of War

One of Rice's seminal and departing actions as Secretary of State was the protection of women and girls within her capacity as Chair of the United Nations Security Council, the principal policy-making body of the United Nations.[59] Representing the United States, Rice advanced the passage of UN Security Council Resolution 1820, which categorized rape as a war crime, a crime against humanity, and a constitutive act of genocide, with the onus on UN member states to investigate and punish perpetrators. 1820 remains a key instrument continuously enforced globally,[60] with June 20 designated as the International Day to Eliminate Sexual Violence in Conflict.

The data around the prevalence of sexual violence in conflict is troubling. According to a UN report, 1,429 incidents of gender-based violence (GBV) were reported in the Democratic Republic of Congo (DRC) in one 12-month period, and 68% of survivors of these atrocities were children. Indeed, there is a worldwide scourge of rape as a weapon of war. This has been documented in Bosnia, Sri Lanka, the Central African Republic (CAR), and the DRC.

In Yemen, where we have the longest ongoing global humanitarian crisis, there has been a 70% increase in reports of sexual violence, including rape. The UN estimates that in conflict zones, for every one rape that is reported, between 10 and 20 rapes are not. A troubling fact is that perpetrators can be military officers, local security forces, militants, civilians, or workers in displacement camps. Rape and sexual violence are often designed to demoralize and humiliate victims and spread fear and paranoia in communities.

Girl-child survivors face immense stigma because of the cultural significance of losing one's virginity through being violated while also being unmarried. Add to that the risk of sexually transmitted infections like HIV/AIDS. In South Sudan, 2,300 cases of sexual violence, including rape, gang rape, and sexual slavery, were reported by mid-2018, with 21% of the survivors being children. Children born of rape face multiple problems, including stigmatization, abandonment, and rejection by their community. This increases the risk of these victims seeking alternative communities of acceptance, such as terrorist groups, perpetuating a vicious cycle. Around 6,000 Yazidi women and children were captured and sold into sexual slavery after an attack in 2014 by ISIS fighters.[61]

All these troubling facts drove the rationale behind UNSCR 1820, which concerned itself with the security of women and girls from rape in situations of armed conflict separate and apart from other international measures. For example the CEDAW serves as the global Bill of Rights for women, UNSCR 1325 gives women a voice in peace negotiations, and UNSCR 1794 addresses country-specific perpetration of violence against women. In many ways, 1820 is like the Geneva Convention regarding the treatment of women in war as it relates to sexual violence against women as a threat to global peace and security. Indeed, the Geneva Conventions govern the conduct of actors in war through a set of rules, but 1820 is more assertive on the criminality of rape as a weapon of war.[62]

Specifically, Rice argued that rape was a crime that could never be condoned in war or in peace. For example, women and girls around the world had been subjected to widespread and deliberate acts of sexual violence in the context of peace, where perpetrators can be brought to justice. However, it was not until UNSCR 1820 was passed that perpetrators of rape as a weapon of war could be prosecuted for committing an international crime. The defilement of a woman or girl child is a fatal blow to her personhood. It tears at the domestic and larger community fabric, the rule of law, and the sense of any semblance of security.

Underpinning Rice's political philosophy is the importance of institutions that uphold the rule of law as being at the heart of peace and security. Additionally, effective legislators, lawyers, judges, laws, local and international institutions are at the heart of peace and security for women and girls. For women, equality before the law occurs where global and local institutions exist complementarily, with such institutions working to implement and uphold the rule of law to the fullest.

John Bolton, U.S Ambassador to the UN, George Bush, President of the United States and Condoleezza Rice, U.S. Secretary of State (left to right) attend a High Level Plenary Meeting at the UN Security Council on Sept. 15, 2005 regarding terrorism. (UPI Photo/Ezio Petersen)

Rice's political philosophy as a woman working on global peace and security is illuminated in some of her earlier writings. Her body of work related to her expertise in Soviet military and political power dynamics, also positioned her as a respected academic and a sought-after Soviet expert.

One of her earlier writings, "The Soviet Union and the Czechoslovak Army, 1948-1983: Uncertain Allegiance," provides an analysis of Rice's exposure to the power dynamics that shaped the Soviet Union. It also offers us a glimpse into her views on global political power dynamics. In this book, she delves into the domestic dimensions of East European Party-Military relations, explores institutions and designations of the Czechoslovak armed forces and their Soviet counterparts, and analyzes Soviet and party policy instruments.

According to Rice, as it relates to the relationship between the military and political party in power, in that region, the relative in-balance of power in Party-Military relations resulted from a political phenomenon she describes as "military clientage" to political leaders. It is where the Czechoslovak People's Army stood suspended between the Czechoslovak nation and the socialist world order, bringing to fore the tensions that wedged allegiance from 1969 to 1983, an era that was critical for that region's standing globally.[63]

Contextualized, when it comes to peace and security, the military plays a critical role as a guarantor of regime security and the community's security, where women and girls tend to be the most vulnerable. However, the military's role must always be tempered by democratic principles and documents such as constitutions, legislation, policies, and institutions that work to enforce and uphold the citizens' unalienable rights.

Clarity of Leadership

Drawing upon Rice's analysis of Eastern Europe, there is a nexus between the local political-military culture, reactions, and attitudes towards adequately fighting violent extremism, violence against women and girls, the presence and role of women in the military, and how these considerations combined can foster discourse in the effective protection of women and girls in war and in peace. For example, in Syria, North Eastern Nigeria, Colombia, and the Philippines, to name a few, violence persists because of the tensions between the military, the party in power, non-state actors, rebels, and violent extremist groups who pose a threat to the national security of these nation-states. How different would the discourse be if women had more prominent roles in the military, at peace negotiations, and during the creation of founding documents and institutions in their respective nations? The significance of a woman's intellectual primacy and perspective as it relates to military and political power concerning peace and security should not be overlooked. Indeed, during my interview of Dr. Rice, she underscored how the prominent roles of women foreign ministers for example, enabled them a seat at the table at the UN to champion economic empowerment and ending violence against women and girls.[64]

Another critical piece of work that sheds light upon some of Rice's political and military thought leadership and philosophy is in one of the earlier publications she co-authored with Philip Zelikow, entitled "Germany Unified and Europe Transformed: A Study in Statecraft."[65] There, Rice's analysis can be summed up as follows: there are lessons in statecraft that can guide policymakers, including anticipating the unexpected as encapsulated in the East German exodus in the Summer of 1989. At times, it is imperative to choose optimal goals, even if they seem politically infeasible or inconvenient. Such was the case during the integration of Germany into the Soviet Bloc, notwithstanding Soviet objections. Clarity of a government's objectives portends the possibility of achieving the said objective as showcased by Washington and Bonn, something Moscow failed to do.[66] In other words, governments must exercise political will and be willing to roll up their sleeves to put in the work that will help facilitate systemic change. Indeed, this kind of commitment is very crucial for the protection and empowerment of women and girls.

Other insights that emerge from the book are whether when it came to reunification, the stabilization of an intolerable situation, or outright revolutionary change as the precondition for engagement is the approach. This is a thought-provoking question that ought to be asked in the context of the role women and girls can play in bringing peace and security. Is the best approach stabilization, outright revolutionary change, or a combination of both?

According to Rice, today's world order is fraught with political agendas and ideologies. Thus, efforts and exercises in democracy are like growing pains and must not be abandoned. The world order often reflects the world's citizens grappling to find themselves, as we have seen in the Middle East and North Africa. Therefore, offers Rice, we ought to applaud the natural yearning for self-determination, even if rocky, as we have seen in Afghanistan, Iraq, Syria, Egypt, Turkey and the democratic revolutionary activities happening globally. One of the most popular ones is the convening day after day, and month after month, at Tahrir Square in Cairo, where citizens held political demonstrations that birthed the 2011 Egyptian revolution. Everyone saw the demonstrations on the news and the resignation of President Hosni Mubarak, with women playing a central role.[67] Similarly, in Liberia, women played an instrumental role during peace talks. Specifically, the work of the activists in the Women of Liberia Mass Action for Peace catalyzed the end of the Second Liberian Civil War in 2003 and the resignation of President Charles Taylor.[68]

Fairness and Equality

Civil unrest in Tahrir Square, Cairo, Egypt, 1st Feb 2011. Thousands of people have been protesting against President Hosni Mubarak.
Contributor: Trinity Mirror / Mirrorpix

Rice, in her book "Democracy: Stories from the Long Road to Freedom," discusses how the balance of power that favors fairness and equality facilitates peace and security. In the book, she analyses the succession of events involving citizens exercising their democratic rights of freedom of speech, to congregate and to protest as "Exhibit A" of for example freedom's awakening in the Middle East as "the people" seek to speak truth to justice and exercise their inalienable rights.[69] Rice proffers that though some may argue there were no clear dividends of democracy from the Arab Spring, others would argue the process alone, of a people seeking to have their democratic rights upheld by telling their side of the story through protest and activism, though confusing and terrifying as it may seem to an outsider, provide a glimmer of hope in the possibilities of the future. Some would even say it was a cathartic experience for the Egyptian people. I must say that I was inspired by the voices of the people, especially women raising their voices in Tahrir Square. Indeed, so was one of my best friends who named her daughter in honor of that movement. As Rice's book title indicates, democracy is not overnight, but an organic phenomenon with the culmination of many small and big efforts that form its DNA.

Likewise, the suffragists' resilient efforts and those of their supporters across the globe to achieve equality for women vis-a-vis the right to vote, be educated, own property, and other inalienable rights may have seemed slow-moving. However, these efforts were not wasted, as they inch-by-inch chipped away at inequality and culminate into the becoming of the women's movement, in general, and empowered individual women, specifically, who strove towards their own self-determination and thus inspired a generation of women and girls.

The Dividends of Democracy

Across the globe, away from the Middle East, in North America, the possibilities and dividends of democracy were in the making and on the verge of being realized almost five decades prior to the Arab Spring. It is where Rice was a youth growing up in Birmingham, Alabama, where African-Americans grappled with securing their inalienable rights vis-a-vis the civil rights movement. Indeed, legislative measures, catalyzed by impact litigation, were passed to achieve the objectives espoused in the Universal Declaration of Human Rights and the U.S. Constitution. Post-slavery and the Civil War, persons of African descent in America found themselves fighting for their destiny towards peace, equality, and democracy, which the status quo and the institutions were clearly not going to give away freely. Evidence of this was a woman at the forefront of this movement, Rosa Parks, who refused to give up her seat to a white passenger as well as the Montgomery bus boycott in Alabama, a state where Rice grew up.[70] This imagery of a black woman taking a seat boldly at that time in history is a sight of inspiration.

Though continents apart, the Civil Rights Movement and Arab Spring, juxtaposed, have a common thread: speaking truth to justice and civil disobedience as recipes for a democratic society. It is no surprise that Rice would have a unique frame of reference as a woman of color working on U.S. national and global security issues. Indeed, as a little girl of color, Rice went to school and was friends with one of the four little girls who were bombed by the KKK in her hometown of Birmingham, Alabama.[71]

Whereas the Arab Spring may embody efforts at democracy and the intense challenges that could occur during this process, the Civil Rights movement represented the realization of some of the dividends of democracy and the intense challenges that can occur during this part of the process. These two unique parts of the sum of the constitutional DNA of democracy are teachable elements for future efforts in upholding the rights of women and girls in the context of peace and security, and the role women such as Rice can play in bringing this to bear when given a seat at the table. This is demonstrated in her role in championing UN Security Council Resolution 1820 and the world's responsibility to protect women and girls in war, whether during the Arab Spring, during the Civil Rights movement, or in the Democratic Republic of Congo (DRC).

In Rice's memoir, "Extraordinary, Ordinary People: A Memoir of Family," we get a glimpse into the impact of being the daughter of educators, the role of the church on her life, and Rice's family support for and involvement in the Civil Rights movement. We also learn about Rice's remarkable career as Provost at Stanford University in Palo Alto, California at a young age, and how her family background, complemented her political and diplomatic philosophy, and how these factors shaped who she became as a diplomat on behalf of the American people.[72]

"You are well-prepared for whatever is ahead of you,"[73] were words that were spoken to Rice as the only child of her parents. Notably, these are similar words Vice President Harris indicated she was raised with by her mother in Oakland, California.

Since half the battle is in the mind, there is no arguing that these words anchored the person Rice became. Indeed, she went on to be the first at many great opportunities where any person would feel intimidated and unprepared. Her parents gave her a seat at the table at the "golden hour"[74] of her life – her formative years – enabling her to form her voice and identity, and exercise her self-determination, including taking the road less taken, and inspiring women and girls to soar on roads less taken.

Another seminal moment that shaped Rice's thinking was her early exposure to equality of the sexes as embodied in her parents' mutual decision for her father, and not her mother, to leave the school system where both her parents had been teaching before they got married; this was due to an anti-nepotism rule which barred spouses from teaching at the same educational institution. According to Rice, when she inquired of her parents on what drove their decision, her father informed her that her mother had been at the school longer, and that it was only fair that *he* move to another school. This action signaled fairness to a young Rice, as well as reinforce her equal worth to her peers regardless of gender.

As though the universe, or better yet God Almighty, was signaling to me that I was on the right path during my research for this manifesto, as my stars will have it, like my meeting RBG, I had the privilege of meeting Rice in Washington, DC at the National Book Festival in the Fall of 2017. That same year the Women, Peace and Security Act was passed in the U.S. Congress. This literary festival founded by former U.S. First Lady Laura Bush and James H. Billington, is organized annually by the U.S. Library of Congress. It is a Disneyland for book lovers with the book talks representing different theme parks. I parked my car nearby so that I could offload my purchases in my trunk in between coffee breaks. Rice was present to discuss her book "Democracy: Stories from the Long Road to Freedom" (Democracy).

In "Democracy," Rice discusses the well-documented transitions and efforts by nations to transition to democracies in the 90s. Some of the examples she gives include Poland, through the movements of Solidarity under the leadership of Lech Walçsa; Romania, where power was wrested from the hands of Nicolae Ceausescu; the Balkans, owing to the breakup of Yugoslavia; and Russia before Vladimir Putin, at the end of the Cold War between the United States and the Soviet Union, catalyzing consolidated democracies in Eastern Europe and everywhere in between. As a reader, the key takeaway is the complexity and sometimes slow-moving crystallization of elements of democracy globally from the Middle-East to Africa and everywhere in between.[75] In other words, democracy takes patience and persistence. From Egypt to Yemen and the Black Lives Matter Movement, we see how activism and movements produce women leaders and political change.

Islamic Cleric

Rice recalls in "Democracy" her encounter with the granddaughter of an Iraqi cleric who paid her a visit in D.C. According to Rice, the young lady informed her that she wanted to be a foreign minister like Rice. There is something remarkable and unremarkable about an Iraqi girl being inspired by an African-American woman. Remarkable in that Rice was shaping the becoming of a young Middle Eastern girl, continents from the United States and a great distance from Rice's beginnings in Alabama. Unremarkable because since time immemorial, when women succeed, they naturally inspired and improved their nuclear and extended communities for the better.

My grandmother Alhaja Nimotallahi in Nigeria was the daughter of an Islamic cleric who could recite the Al Quran from beginning to end. Thus, this story resonated quite deeply with me. As Rice described the young Iraqi girl, what flashed in my mind was my grandmother as a young woman, wanting to experience self-determination in the early 1930s. According to my grandmother, she was not allowed to receive the free western education offered by the British colonials for fear of children being kidnapped and sold into slavery. I could not help but wonder, what if my grandmother had the same experience of being aware of a Condoleezza Rice, a Madam C.J. Walker or RBG, much like the Iraqi girl had? Had she heard of Chief Olufunmilayo Ransome Kuti's work on women and girls' empowerment in Nigeria? Would she too have aspired to become a Suffragist, foreign minister, lawyer or even a business tycoon, with the Islamic education she received? Could she have succeeded in the society she lived in, or would she have had to settle for her daughter accomplishing the dreams she was denied because of her gender, just like RBG's mother Celia did? What role could technology have played in her access to different perspectives? Today, more than before, technology is connecting women with each other and facilitating their mobilization efforts.

Drawing the parallels of inspiration across cultures and continents underscores that women and girls ought to, and can, draw inspiration and strength from people who do and do not look like them, share their cultural heritage or political views. This just goes to show how one girl, or one woman, can have an impact on the lives of so many others. The fact is that our global society is interconnected. Given this reality, giving women the platform, leadership exposure, and experience can shape the civic becoming or DNA of people, communities, and even movements. Rice's impact is seen not just through an international lens but also through organizations such as Girls Incorporated and Ban Bossy, an organization that encourages girls to lead-where she influences young minds of up and coming women leaders to take a seat at the table, lean in, and lead with grace and distinction. [76] She also carries on her legacy of mentorship at Stanford University as a professor, thought leader, and Director of the Hoover Institution.

There is a saying attributed to the late poet Maya Angelou that although we may not remember what people say to us, we will remember how they make us feel. Like RBG, when I met Rice, what struck me the most was not just her brilliance and physical beauty but her beautiful spirit, which was overwhelmingly present. Although our meeting was short, it was delightful and unforgettable for me, and she agreed to chat with me about my research topic at a later time. She kept her word, notwithstanding not knowing me previously, and given her status in society, she did not have to make time to guide me. Yet she did and inspired me to keep writing this manifesto to completion, giving me a seat at the table.

The right words at the right time are like marrow to the bone, and so were Rice's words of encouragement for my research.

Subsequently, I was fortunate to have multiple phone conversations with Rice, thanks to the amazing coordination of her support staff at Stanford University, to get her insights on my research related to UNSCR 1325 and why we needed more women at the table. The greatest takeaway was her guidance and challenge that I thoroughly research the companions of 1325, such as UNSCR 1820, on the criminalization of rape as a weapon of war, and understand how these measures together fortify efforts around the protection of women and girls. Following her counsel, my further research led me to discover that Resolutions 1325, 1820, 1794, and a few other global measures were imperative for operationalizing the CEDAW (AKA the Bill of Rights for Women), because they tackled head-on the issue of violence against women in various contexts. In the case of 1820, which Rice saw to fruition during her role as Secretary of State within the Obama Administration transition, rape as a weapon of war was deemed an international war crime, and UN Member States were explicitly urged to investigate and prosecute perpetrators to the fullest of the law. This was a clear signal to governments and citizens that never again would sexual crimes against women and girls be tolerated because of an ongoing war or conflict. 1820 occurred at a "golden hour" where in countries like the Democratic Republic of Congo (DRC), various unsavory actors, were utilizing rape as a tactical weapon of war. There could not have been a more timely point in history for 1820. And it remains so relevant as our world continues to be fraught with sexual violence, war, disease, and climate disaster, all of which exacerbate the physical, food, and health security of women and girls. Rice's remarkable life story and the work of her hands come full circle as she blossomed from a young girl traumatized by the murder of four of her classmates due to racial violence to a woman of purpose whose legacy includes protecting women and girls from violence and inspiring women and girls from all walks of life.

Part 3

WOMEN, GIRLS AND MOVEMENTS FOR THE PEOPLE

Zozibini Tunzi, of South Africa, is crowned Miss Universe by her predecessor, Catriona Gray of the Philippines, at the 2019 Miss Universe pageant at Tyler Perry Studios in Atlanta, Georgia, U.S. December 8, 2019. REUTERS/Elijah Nouvelage TPX IMAGES OF THE DAY

Beauty, Resilience and Self-Determination: Ms. World and South African Zozibini Tunzi

Women of African descent are gradually chipping away at the Venus Hortentot curse, where they are viewed as helpless savages or objectified in the most disturbing way that is an assault to their personhood and self-determination.[77] In 1810, Venus Hortentot, also referred to as Sara Baartman, was enslaved and trafficked from South Africa to London around when she was 20 years old. She was exhibited as an exotic freak in circuses and other private venues for five years before she died in 1815. She was sold many times, including to a French doctor who dissected her body and had it displayed in museums in France. Owing to the efforts of the late President Nelson Mandela, her remains were returned home to South Africa in 2002. She was buried 187 years after she departed her homeland against her will.[78]

On December 8, 2019, South African beauty contestant, Zozibini Tunzi, was crowned Ms. Universe at Tyler Perry Studios in Atlanta, Georgia. What impact can a beautiful woman of African descent have on the universe? There is something ironic about Tunzi's crowning especially in light of her active distinction of her beauty from the Eurocentric perception of beauty. In essence, her beauty, intellect, and pageant platform on combatting violence against women defies what triggered the objectification of Sarah Baartman over 200 years ago. She embodies everything Sarah was not afforded the opportunity to be: intelligent, beautiful, political, glamorous, self-affirming, unapologetic, empowering, soft, tough, complex and human.

According to the UN CEDAW, women have the inalienable right to all human rights delineated in the United Nations Charter in addition to other important UN measures. One of these rights is a woman's right to peace in her womanhood and protection from violent words and/or actions against her personhood. Carrying out the mandate of CEDAW, Tunzi defines beauty and used her platform as a beauty queen to address social policy issues; specifically, gender-based violence and the imperative of grooming girls to become leaders and active agents in their self-determination, regardless of their status in society.[79]

Violence

The daughter of educators from a modest community in South Africa, Tunzi's natural African beauty and passion for giving women a platform captivates our imagination. It also drew our attention to the scourge of violence against women in Africa. The issue of violence against women in Africa perpetrated by Africans and non-Africans has been taboo in African society. The community has not yet fully grappled with this issue. Thus, Tunzi's literal parade of the issue by wearing an outfit made from thousands of letters written by survivors, supporters, and perpetrators shifted the narrative of violence against women onto a global platform and catalyzed discourse around needed changes.[80]

Additionally, as part of her women's empowerment focus during her Crown, Tunzi has pledged her commitment to empower girls to own their voice. Indeed, during the question and answer portion of the competition, when asked: "What is the most important thing we should teach young girls today?" Tunzi replied:

"I think the most important thing we should be teaching young girls today is leadership. It's something that has been lacking in young girls and women for a very long time, not because we don't want to, but because of what society has labeled women to be. I think we are the most powerful beings in the world and that we should be given every opportunity and that is what we should be teaching these young girls, to take up space, nothing is as important as 'taking up space' in society and cementing yourself, thank you."[81]

Tunzi's message was very relevant and has been a long time coming, especially across Africa, where violence against women and girls is prevalent. Indeed, Nobel Peace Laureate and President Ellen Johnson Sirleaf of Liberia, along with many other women, helped put the pieces together in Liberia after decades of conflict and violence, a remarkable feat in peacemaking. However, what is even more impressive about President Sirleaf are the obstacles she overcame as a woman, including surviving and departing a violent marriage (as she shared in her autobiography), and still becoming the first female President in Africa, first female President of Liberia, and serving as a key person in the reconstruction of Liberia after its second civil war and during the Ebola crisis.[82]

Tunzi's ability to understand the weight of her platform in tackling important issues affecting women in general, and African women specifically, is encapsulated in her responses to her questions during the beauty competition question and answer session. Her responses provide us with a glimpse into her consciousness. For instance, on the issue of climate change, the host asked her, "Are leaders of today doing enough to protect future generations from climate change? If not, what more should they be doing?" Her answer: "I think that the future leaders could do a little bit more. However, I feel like we, as individuals ourselves, could also play a part in making the climate the way it should be in the future. Children are protesting for the climate, and I feel like adults should join as well, and corporations should join as well. The government should take it seriously. I mean, since 6th grade, I have been learning that the climate is deteriorating, and the planet is dying. It is up to us to keep our planet safe. Thank you."[83]

Show Up to the Table as Your Authentic Self

Part of women taking a seat at the table and shaping the discourse also includes showing up as their authentic selves. For each woman, authenticity will be different, but it is often what amplifies the space they occupy. For example, Tunzi stood out because she embraced her humble roots from a modest village in South Africa and made the very intentional and conscious decision to wear her hair natural, without the additional extensions that beauty queens are often encouraged to wear. The decision was made while existing in a world of beauty where all such resources were at her disposal. Indeed, part of finding and solidifying one's identity is charting a new course and being the trailblazer. In a lot of ways, Tunzi's actions sent the catalytic message to women and girls who share her racial identity that you can be natural, beautiful, and an activist for the rights of women and girls, all at once. It also serves as a rewiring of societal thinking on the standards of beauty and platforms for advocacy, helping to broaden the research around strategies for fostering peace and security in society.

Another curious aspect of Tunzi's platform is this ever-growing pressure and burden that women bear to keep up the veneer of steel strength, rather than being comfortable in their skin and showing their femininity and humanity for fear of looking weak. Underlying this dangerous assumption is the conclusion that because women are strong and resilient, which they are, they should accept the rigors of violence upon their spirits, souls, and bodies as the norm. Also, Tunzi wearing one of her outfits made from 2,000 letters against violence against women, highlights key elements of 1325, including engaging males when she challenged men to take up the mantle as allies in ending violence against women and girls, and to co-partner with women in creating a safe and secure society.[84]

All Eyes on Hollywood

In Tunzi's words, "nothing is as important as taking up space in society and cementing yourself."[85] Tunzi's platform is a challenge to the fashion, entertainment, and image industry in the power they hold in tackling societal inequality and ending the perpetuation of violence against women and girls through various artistic depictions. They need only to exercise the political will. Indeed, some in the entertainment industry are already using their powerful platform, as we will see in the TIME'S UP movement discussed later in the manifesto. Also, Tunzi's African beauty is a clarion call that there is economic power when industry markets reflect the real world. Indeed, there is an untapped customer base of women of color through Tunzi's brand of showing up as her authentic self at the table. It goes without saying that Tunzi is beautiful but her declaration of her beauty through her words and actions amplified her beauty and impact on the world.

Much like Funmilayo, RBG, and Rice, education and knowledge, when imparted to a girl, positively impacts the individual and society as a whole. When women win, our world wins. Like Miriam Makeba, the late renowned South African entertainer, who used her platform to fight apartheid, Tunzi works towards the important issue of combatting violence against women and girls. During the COVID-19 crisis, where societies were on lockdown, her policy initiative could not have been more timely. Perhaps like the biblical Queen Esther, she was created for such a time, where silence is not an option, and using her crown saves lives.[86]

Education and Violence: Pakistani Girls Education Activist Malala Yousafzai

U.S. President Barack Obama, First Lady Michelle Obama, and their daughter Malia meet with Malala Yousafzai, the young Pakistani schoolgirl who was shot in the head by the Taliban in the Oval Office of the White House Oct. 11, 2013 in Washington, DC. Contributor: White House Photo / Alamy Stock Photo

On October 9, 2012, a Taliban gunman shot Malala Yousafzai in the head as she rode home on a bus after her exams at her school in Pakistan's Swat Valley. She was targeted because she campaigned for education.

Yousafzai survived her brutal attack, won the Nobel Peace Prize, created the Malala Fund to empower girls to learn and lead, and acquired her Philosophy, Politics and Economics degree from the University of Oxford.[87]

After a Gun Shot in the Head

The seminal moments that ushered my foray into how violent extremism adversely impacts women and girls was first at a college event where the speakers discussed rape as a weapon of war in the DRC and second a news report presented by Democracy Now! on the brutal assassination of former Pakistani Prime Minister Benazir Bhutto. She was the first woman to hold the office, and it happened in her home country of Pakistan. The images of her waiving from her motorcade moments before she was gunned down stayed with me forever and left an indelible mark upon me. I was keenly aware of terrorism in America in light of the 9/11 attacks. But a female leader being targeted and bombed by terrorists was something I had not heard of in my adult life. Unfortunately, this was a preview of the spate of subsequent brazen violence against girls and women we would witness. These included a violent gun attack upon Yousafzai, a Pakistani youth education activist, the kidnapping of 276 female students from a secondary school in the town of Chibok in North-Eastern Nigeria, and the assassination of Berta Cáceres, a Honduran environmental activist.

Indeed, Bhutto's father was also brutally assassinated previously. These facts, combined with successive events, such as the insurgency of the Taliban in the region and female suicide bombers being used as pawns for terroristic schemes, caused me to pay attention to what was happening related to the safety and security of women and girls globally. Five years after Bhutto's assassination, I was in Washington, D.C. on my drive to work. While listening to Democracy Now!, I learned that the Taliban shot a teenage girl named Malala Yousafzai in the head on her way from school in Swat Valley, Pakistan. According to news reports, Yousafzai was targeted because of her activism around girls' education. Her attackers considered her to be a threat because she advocated for the enlightenment of the minds of girls. When I heard of the attack on Yousafzai, I had a flashback to the attack on Bhutto and remember thinking to myself, "What in the world is going on in the world?" In the same breath, I recall thinking what a brave girl Yousafzai was fighting for a cause in an environment where girls' education was considered an abomination at that time in history. Undoubtedly, it takes an enormous amount of courage to face the patriarchal establishment and challenge the status quo. Indeed, Yousafzai's courage served as an inspiration to people across the globe.

In her book, "I am Malala: The Girl Who Stood Up for Education and Was Shot By the Taliban," Yousafzai writes that her mission and life's calling is to foster a world where girls and boys can exercise their inalienable right to be educated. Her story inspires us to believe that gender, culture, and religion do not have to be stumbling blocks to making an impact in the world.

When I heard of Yousafzai's attack, it was hard for me not to be inspired by her bravery. I say this because this was a very hectic time in my professional life as a young lawyer. Thus, I continued to track her recovery and reports of whether her attackers were brought to justice. Indeed, there is something empowering about seeing someone fighting for what is right coming out triumphant. And in the case of Yousafzai, this is especially so where she not only recovers from the assault on her spirit, soul and body, she doubles down on her life's calling on education for young people.

As an active member and co-chair of the International Law Committee of the American Bar Association Young Lawyers Division (YLD), Yousafzai's courage and passion inspired me to draft a resolution for consideration by my colleagues in the YLD General Assembly on the Convention on the Rights of the Child (CRC). The resolution highlighted youth trafficking in the U.S. and the kidnapping of 276 schoolgirls by

Boko Haram in North-Eastern Nigeria, just for wanting to be educated like Malala. Luckily, I was supported by colleagues who helped shepherd the resolution to passage.[88]

The UN Convention on the Rights of the Child (CRC)

The CRC states that the right to education is a fundamental, inalienable right of every child worldwide. The CRC is a global covenant and is one which 196 nations have ratified, acceding to the CRC's provisions and articles. According to the United Nations International Children's Emergency Fund (UNICEF), the CRC is one of the most ratified international treaties, providing guidance on young people's rights globally. However, the United States has not ratified the Convention.

With 54 provisions, the CRC delineates the international consensus around the protection of young people across the globe. Pursuant to the CRC, a child is a person of 18 years and under and with inalienable rights including, but not limited to 1) the right to a name and nationality; 2) access to education and healthcare, and 3) freedom of thought and speech.[89]

The CRC is the grandchild of the Geneva Declaration on the Rights of the Child of 1924 and is the offspring of the UN Universal Declaration of Human Rights of 1948 and the UN Universal Declaration on the Rights of the Child of 1959. The protection of children is referenced in numerous other multilateral measures such as the Convention Against Torture and other Cruel, Inhumane or Degrading Treatment or Punishment of 1987, the International Covenant on Civil, and Political Rights and the International Covenant on Economic, Social and Cultural Rights of 1976. However, the CRC is the international promise that focuses on nurturing children in the global society.

The CRC's need was conceived in Poland in 1978 as U.N. member states deliberated initiatives for 1979 – a year it dubbed the "International Year of the Child." Moving forward, between 1979 and 1989, a working group was convened to draft the text of the CRC, and on September 1990, the CRC entered into force.

Yousafzai's activism breathes life into the spirit and intent of the CRC, much like Greta Thunberg now does for the Paris Agreement. Education and planet protection are crucial for the survival of women and girls, and that of humanity.

Indeed, it was because of her local activism around education, and her communication with the global media such as through her blogging on BBC online in her Diary of a Pakistani schoolgirl on the importance of protecting girls' education, that Yousafzai helped expose the violence and threat of violence by extremist groups against children seeking education. Unfortunately, this was also one of the reasons Yousafzai was brutally assaulted and attacked.

Like many activists, by the time Yousafzai was shot in the head, which houses her brain, which enables her to acquire knowledge, she had already mobilized many around the importance of girls' education and had earned her accolades locally. Her attackers failed to contemplate in their evil plans how the attack would either make a martyr out of Yousafzai had she died or mobilize her supporters further and provide her with an even larger platform to rally support around her cause if she survived. Fortunately for the world, what the terrorists meant for evil, God turned around for good. Now, a boarding schoolgirl in North-Eastern Nigeria can be inspired by Yousafzai's story of resilience, rehabilitation, and the fight for education.

Yousafzai has built her legacy through speaking truth to justice and the power of the pen and words. She has since been honored as a Nobel Peace Prize winner, refusing to allow herself to be deterred by the Taliban's attacks.

In her book, "I Am Malala," Yousafzai writes about wanting to grow taller. Little did she know that the height she would reach would surpass anything that her mind could have ever imagined. Owing to Yousafzai's work, numerous efforts were undertaken to make girls' education a global imperative. For example, the Obama Administration initiative, implemented by USAID, State Department, and Peace Corps called "Let Girls Learn." Through this initiative, we see how U.S. soft power complements grassroots efforts to foster peace, security, and investment in economic empowerment globally through girls' education in at-risk communities where violent extremism may be festering. Additionally, in my previous role as a foreign affairs staffer on Capitol Hill, part of my portfolio included working with other staff members on mobilizing non-partisan support for Malala to receive the Congressional Gold Medal.

Indeed, studies have shown that where girls are educated, a country's GDP increases, early marriages and female genital mutilation/cutting decrease, and there is a spur in the community's innovation.[90]

Yousafzai, and the other women discussed in this manifesto, are "Exhibit A" of the return on the investment in girls' education. As an example, we see how the Malala Fund has empowered girls through education in Afghanistan, Brazil, India, Nigeria, Pakistan, and the Syria region. Imagine the multiplier effect and the impact the girls inspired by Yousafzai can have in the world!

In her book, speeches, and other writings, Yousafzai often references her Islamic faith as encouraging the acquisition of knowledge, no matter who you are. This runs contrary to the argument often advanced by extremist groups who attribute the acquisition of knowledge to Western civilization and see knowledge acquired by women and girls as something to be frowned upon. Hearing about the importance of education and how her religion promotes the acquisition of knowledge from a young Muslim woman is not only empowering but also enlightens us about what we already knew deep in our hearts and souls. God, Allah, or whatever we choose to call the creator of the universe, wants us to acquire wisdom, knowledge, and understanding. As Malala aptly puts it, the higher power promotes our acquisition of knowledge and wisdom so that we can fully experience all of the wonderful things that have been created for us to appreciate through the senses with which we are equipped.[91]

In 2014, Yousafzai was honored with the Nobel Peace Prize, making her the youngest recipient of this esteemed award at that time. Her acceptance speech captures the beauty of an educated mind, the product of which has borne her passion for girls' education and provides an intimate insight into how the acquisition of knowledge and wisdom has amplified Yousafzai's character. Hear this young mind from Mingora, Pakistan, address a room full of adults in Oslo, Norway, just a little over two years after she was shot in the head for advocating for girls' education and you will find your sense of hope and resilience flying on the wings of possibility.[92]

Wings to Fly All the Way to the Nobel Peace Prize

On December 10, 2014, in Oslo, Norway,[93] we heard the words, "Bismillah hir rahman ir rahim. In the name of God, the most merciful, the most beneficent," the first words uttered by Yousafzai. She said this just before she beautifully and gracefully painted the picture of the seminal events that shaped her, and positioned her for a seat at the table as a Noble Laureate for peace.

First, we learned about her nuclear family and the love her parents poured into her, especially her father. For this, she thanked him for not clipping her wings but letting her fly. Next, she thanked her mother and teachers who taught her to be true and brave. This is reminiscent of the character described in the Ballad of Mulan where a premodern Chinese heroine and woman warrior was encouraged by prescient people around her to be brave and true to her values, inner core, and embrace the trailblazer she was created to be.[94]

Like the mythical Mulan from the Chinese dynasties,[95] embodying women's abilities and equality, Yousafzai's remarkable story portends that there will be books written and movies made about her life, as she appears to be living out her destiny and her life true to the Pakistani legend she was named after—the inspirational Malalai of Maiwand who is the Pashtun Joan of Arc.

Additionally, she dedicated her award and the accompanying cash prize to youth education, and doubled down on her commitment to stand up for youth rights, raise their voices, and empower rather than pity them. She challenged the world to take action "so it becomes the last time that we see a child deprived of education," especially the 66 million girls who are deprived of education globally.[96] Yousafzai's passionate plea for the protection of the right to education comes from her personal experience of witnessing over 400 schools destroyed in her community, where suddenly education went from being a right to a crime - and girls were precluded from going to school. Faced with this dangerous reality, Yousafzai had the option to keep silent and wait to be killed; the second option was to speak up, and be killed. She noted "I chose the second one; I decided to speak up."[97]

She bravely took a seat at the table to defend her own right, and the rights of millions of youth to education and launched a movement for education that is now impacting all corners of the world. Yousafzai challenges us to "become the first generation that decides to be the last which sees empty classrooms, lost childhoods, and wasted potentials."[98]

Climate and Violence: Planet Advocate Greta Thunberg

On August 20, 2018, a Swedish ninth grader named Greta Thunberg began her civil disobedience by not attending school to camp outside of the Swedish Parliament to call for stronger action on climate change by holding up a sign reading: *Skolstrejk för klimatet* (School Strike for Climate). Owing to her activism and community organizing around protecting the planet, Thunberg was named Time Magazine's person of the year and has since addressed world leaders on issues related to protecting the planet. This included a speech at the 2020 World Economic Forum and another at a 2019 UN climate change gathering.[99]

Thunberg inspires us all to believe that gender, age, and what the world may view as a disability do not have to be stumbling blocks to making an indelible mark in the world.

Ella Josephine Baker's Community Organizing and Legacy

My foray into environmental justice was catalysed while in law school, around 2009, when I read a book on community organizing—the intersectionality of economic empowerment for working people and environmental justice. This book was written by Van Jones, Founder of the Ella Baker Center for Human Rights (Ella Baker Center), an organization that impacted the trajectory of my advocacy.

Here is how I found out about the Ella Baker Center, and civil rights activist Ella Josephine Baker.

Ella Josephine Baker (1903-1986), was a lifelong African American civil rights activist from the 1930s until her death in the 1980s. Contributor: Everett Collection Inc.

Right after college, I landed a very well-paying entry level job at a lobbying firm. I got this job thanks to the recommendations I received from my college administrators at the Associated Students Incorporated (ASI) where I had thoroughly enjoyed working as a college leader in various capacities. My entry level job had amazing benefits, free lunches, and the opportunity to meet a lot of interesting people in Sacramento, California's state capital. However, as a former student and community organizer, I felt like a fish out of water. I quit the job less than six months after starting, and I sought out other opportunities more aligned with my interests, including interning with a local newspaper. None of these organizations had the available funding to pay me. So, I moved back home to the Bay Area in California where I discovered and decided to intern for the Ella Baker Center for Human Rights, and the American Civil Liberties Union (ACLU) Northern California - while studying for my Law School Admission Test (LSAT). I was accepted to and completed both internships, because I had a difficult time choosing one over the other. I wanted to be a part of the policy issues that each organization worked on. The opportunities worked out well as two unpaid part time jobs, leaving little to no time for idleness, but a lot time for policy change advocacy and intellectual stimulation!

Between both of these enlightening opportunities, I was exposed to impact litigation which advanced important civil rights at the ACLU, while in parallel, honing my community organizing skills at the Ella Baker Center. I found great fulfilment in both opportunities and was inspired to stay at the local and grassroots level for my law school pursuits. As an idealistic college graduate, I found that I was granted a seat at the table with both opportunities where I was entrusted to assist with important projects. One project involved honoring the late Japanese-American civil rights activist Fred Korematsu, whose 1942 conviction for resisting internment was vacated in 1983, owing to the work of a group of talented and dedicated lawyers.

The ceremony was held during the ACLU-Northern California's annual Bill of Rights Day celebration. With the theme of "Freedom Detained: Yesterday and Today," the event highlighted the connections between the internment of Japanese Americans during World War II, and the targeting of Arab, Muslim, and South Asian immigrants after 9/11.

Simultaneously, the activists at the Ella Baker Center empowered me. I learned about community organizing and driving policy change by shadowing organizers working on the "Books Not Bars" initiative, which sought to stop the construction of one of the U.S.' largest juvenile halls in Oakland's Alameda County. The campaign's community organizing resulted in the county's closure of five of the eight California youth prisons, resulting in an 85% reduction in the youth prison population. The main goal of the initiative, was that more investment in quality education will mitigate the incarceration of young people.[100]

Baker was an African American civil and human rights activist who challenged racism in America, and sexism within the civil rights movement. Her seat at the table was her organizing career spanning over 50 years.[101] Her community organizing style empowered oppressed community members to lead the change that they sought to see. Among other remarkable achievements, she earned the distinguished honor of becoming the highest-ranking woman of the National Association for the Advancement of Colored People (NAACP) at the time. Formed in 1909, the NAACP is a civil rights organization in the United States, founded as an interracial endeavor to advance justice for African-Americans.[102]

Baker also worked alongside Civil Rights leader, Dr. Martin Luther King Jr., as Executive Secretary of his Southern Christian Leadership

Conference (SCLC). The SCLC was instrumental in non-violent actions towards racial equity and equality in America, most notably the Montgomery Bus Boycott of 1955 to 1956, which lasted 381 days, and resulted in the desegregation of the Montgomery and Alabama bus system.[103] Throughout her grassroots community organizing work, she also championed giving women and youth a seat at the table. This was brought to fruition through her work in the Student Non-Violent Coordinating Committee (SNCC) which she helped found at her alma mater, Shaw University, years after graduating with Valedictorian honors.[104]

Owing to her superior community organizing skills, Baker was retained as one of the few organizers for the SCLC mobilization of the 1957 Prayer Pilgrimage for Freedom and the 1958 Crusade for Citizenship. Baker organized a voter registration program to turn out African-American voters for the 1958 and 1960 elections, which were very critical groundwork for subsequent laws that impacted the livelihoods of African-Americans, such as the Civil Rights Act of 1964, the 1965 Voting Rights Act, and the Fair Housing Act of 1968. These were historical pieces of legislation towards ending racial discrimination in America, all signed into law by President Lyndon Baines Johnson.[105]

Along with other organizers, Baker's strategy included voter registration campaigns, identifying community grievances to connect with community members, sharing educational information, engaging churches and grassroots centers, and hosting community gatherings such as the one founded in her honor to underscore the importance of civic engagement and the right to vote. The life of Baker serves as an inspiration for me, Van Jones, and others. We recognize her example of how a woman given a seat at the table can inspire women and men alike. Indeed, staying true to Baker's organizing strategy of local empowerment, Jones went on to found and co-found numerous grassroots centers including the organization, "Green for All." One of the initiatives of "Green for All" is Jones' book entitled "The Green Collar Economy: How One Solution Can Fix Our Two Biggest Problems." In the book, Jones who also advised President Obama on this matter, explores the opportunity to save people from poverty and protect our planet through the creation of working class jobs that impact energy conservation. These roles include services to insulate homes, or to increase the utilization of alternative energy sources such as solar panels. Jones argues that this approach gives people a sense of purpose, while earning a living because they are part of a larger cause within their community. They become essential to helping solve a problem which was of most imminent harm to them, and to similarly situated people in the Global South.

However, women and girls tend to have even less access to the opportunities that Jones argued for in his book. Women and girls are also more adversely affected by climate change, due to the destruction of infrastructures that allow access to education and economic empowerment and the absence of their voices during the political discourses that shape their governments' position on climate policy. These among other issues directly impact the destinies of women and girls.[106] Jones' community organizing efforts inspired by Ella Baker fortify Thunberg's efforts today, especially in communities of color. Perhaps the biblical saying "out of the mouth of babes"[107] may prevail on the moral imperative that the global community, without delay, must move the needle on protecting our planet so that we can protect everyone, especially underserved communities and future generations. The global communities grappling with COVID-19, is a sombre reminder of what can happen when we are not proactive, responsible, and vigilant in our actions and decisions. A key argument that Thunberg and Jones marshal, is the urgent need for a safe world for all. This paired with the intersectionality of environmental, health, economic, and racial equity, underscores the adverse impacts on members of the Global South, as well as the most marginalized groups, such as women and girls.

Thunberg's lobbying of the Swedish Parliament during her School Strike for Climate led to over four million youth and other supporters convening global events to bring attention to political inaction on the issue of global warming.[108] Like Thunberg, through the support of the Ella Baker Center for Human Rights and other community organizations, Jones successfully lobbied the U.S. Congress to pass the Green Jobs Act of 2007, authorizing $125 million to train 35,000 people for jobs in the environmental sector. Indeed, Thunberg's activism echoes contentions in Jones' book, which is that as a society continues to neglect its obligation to protect the planet, the people who will suffer the most are the people most in harm's way, including women and girls all over the world, from Oakland, California to Aden, Yemen.

I met Van Jones once at the Ella Baker Center and after introducing myself to him, he expressed how happy he was that I had joined the team, that I would do great and regretted that we would not get to work together because he was on his way to paternity leave. He sounded so giddy to be an expecting dad!

"The Green Collar Economy" sowed a seed and piqued my interest in planet justice. It also motivated me to subsequently draft a research paper on the topic; my research explored the imperative of preserving our biodiversity, and how that in turn preserves people and our humanity - especially since all of us are living organisms and part of an interdependent ecosystem. My independent research findings left an indelible mark upon me that frankly laid dormant until recently, thanks in part to Thunberg's clarion call.

It is time for our reckoning. Our continuous assault on the planet is causing harm to our economies, health, ecosystem, and the biodiversity that supports and promotes the existence of living organisms. Our human destructive actions towards the planet pose a great danger to us and the ecosystem's continued existence.

Psalms 8:2, "Out of the mouth of babes…": God Put Humans in Charge of the Environment

Greta Thunberg holds a placard reading "School strike for the climate" during a protest outside the Swedish parliament on November 30, 2018.
Contributor: Jasper Chamber

A decade after my awakening vis a vis Jones' book, I am grateful to Thunberg for re-awakening the sleeping giant in all of us. It is also heartening to see the global community drawing the nexus between global peace and our environment. Indeed, Thunberg was recently nominated for the Nobel Peace Prize, according to Norwegian Socialist MP Freddy

André Øvstegård, for launching "a mass movement which [he sees] as a major contribution to peace." He further asserted that "if we do nothing to halt climate change, it will be the cause of wars, conflict, and refugees." With hundreds of thousands dead, and millions sheltered in place, as we globally grapple with COVID-19,[109] Thunberg's community organizing to protect the people and the planet is opportune. For those of us who think we still have time, and that planet protection is not our problem to worry about, it is clear that a public health risk is everyone's problem and can impact every aspect of our lives. The fact that a teenage girl is actively leading change in this space, shows how important it is to empower women and girls. It also underscores that when we do so, there is no telling the limits of their impact! Thunberg was empowered by her community and granted a seat at the table to push for change. Similarly, Baker through her seat at the civil rights table mobilized voting in African American communities to get the vote out, which laid the groundwork for the civil rights legislation of the 1960s-addressing the pressing social policy issues of the day. Baker's legacy also lives on in today's generation of community activists such as Political Leader Stacey Abrams of Georgia[110] as well as male allies, like Van Jones.

Currently, the discourse around planet, climate, and environmental justice has broadened with various voices across political spectrums arguing either for or against proactive action from humanity; the proponents are arguing for the sake of future generations and posterity. Also, underpinning the argument for immediate action is the Paris Agreement for Climate Change, which Thunberg through her community activism helped draw the world's attention to.

But frankly, a law or international agreement is only as good as the paper it is written on if there is no way for enforcement mechanisms to facilitate implementation. Sometimes, the world is lucky to have a messenger to help deliver on an important global message.[111] Indeed, in a time where we are all over stimulated and stressed out by constant media, social media and other forms of sensory engagements which overload us cognitively, Thunberg jolted us out of our inertia, and appealed to something within our souls: the wide-eyed optimistic aspects of childhood, which every human being has experienced at some point.

London, England, UK- March 7, 2020: Million Women Rise march in London. Contributor: Rod Olukoya

Some people have attributed her laser focus to her autism, which Thunberg openly discusses as a superpower. Frankly, I cannot help but be reminded of the biblical saying in 1 Peter 2:7 ". . . Now to you who believe, this stone is precious. But to those who do not believe, the stone the builders rejected has become the capstone…"[112] Her autism caught my personal attention because one of my best friend's daughter was diagnosed with autism. My friend's daughter has a private coach to help her channel her energy and to focus, so that she is not overwhelmed or stressed. Yet, when I interact with her, I am keenly aware of her strong, precocious and independent mind. She is also often irritated by condescending remarks or actions towards her, as if she is telling the world "I am not a victim, my autism is a superpower," reminiscent of Thunberg. Indeed, like Thunberg, this child will be great. These set of indisputable facts also underscore to me that the God that I serve is not a God of errors. In our teeny-weeny human brains, we assume that if someone is born dynamic, that they are born defective. Yet time and time again, God proves us wrong; for His glory of course, and for our amazement as we bear witness to His awesomeness. It is indeed in God's ancient nature to show His passion, awesomeness, and deep love for His planet through a schoolgirl.

What if just like the Biblical Esther,[113] Thunberg was created for such a time as ours, just how God created and raised Yousafzai to bring attention to the attack on girls' education across the globe; Tunzi to bring our attention to violence against women and girls; Rice to bring our attention to rape as a weapon of war; Baker to bring our attention to the sacred right to vote and equality before the law; Funmilayo and RBG to bring our attention to women's equality in all quarters of life? If we observe the parallel, each woman's purpose was like Esther's: to save communities from total annihilation. Indeed, each issue championed by the women is timeless, and resonates with all generations and all walks of life. Hopefully, the legacies of Funmilayo, Baker, RBG, Rice, Tunzi, Yousafzai, and Thunberg, and many others referenced and not referenced in this manifesto, resonate with a generation that can energize the battle worn and aging base, for the protection of our planet and people! It is especially important to acknowledge these women and girls, and the many others who have been the most marginalized in our world. Today, it is heartening to hear of the United Nations' pledge to mainstream gender empowerment into all of its Sustainable Development Goals (SDGs) through 2030.[114]

Much like her predecessors discussed in this manifesto, it is important to note the impact of family on women and girls exercising self-determination. For example, Thunberg is related to Svante August Arrhenius, a leading Swedish scientist and environmentalist who developed the theory of the greenhouse effect, and cited how doubling of carbon dioxide in the atmosphere will increase temperatures by 5°C to 6°C. Svante also received the Nobel Prize for Chemistry in 1903.[115]

Much like Yousafzai and Tunzi, we get to bear witness to Thunberg's work when granted a seat at the table through her activism. Like the others in this manifesto, the story of her life is breath-taking, partly because of her youth, and partly because her sense of purpose is intertwined with being part of something greater than her; this is precisely why she appeals to us all, and we can all see ourselves in Thunberg and the other women. They embody the promise of youth, and the possibilities of an adulthood anchored by a clear North Star; this is paired with a fierce moral imperative to make the world a better place - even when the circumstances are inconvenient or seemingly impossible. Through their actions and words, and righteous indignation towards being labelled, boxed, or stopped, they inspire us and grant us insight into the drivers of bravery in their lives and how they in fact shaped - and continue to shape the discourse in the unique spaces they occupy. This is what happens when women and girls have the space to exercise their voice and agency unapologetically.

Indeed, just as we were able to bear witness to Yousafzai's superior wit during her Nobel Peace Prize speech, we can hear the passion in Thunberg's spirit by listening to her speech at the Climate Conference in Madrid, Spain in 2019,[116] where yet again she challenges us to move forward and resist the temptation to maintain the status quo, through our failure to protect the planet. We must not kick the can down the road, she warns and leave our responsibility to protect future generations, especially at a time when doing so may make us way too late to reverse or mitigate the damage. Planet protection and climate change are global security issues, and disproportionately impact women and girls, because they exacerbate existing inequalities related to education, child marriage, violence of all forms, sexual and reproductive health, to name a few. It is notable that only two percent of National Climate Strategies mention girls.[117]

Say It: Our Planet, Our Future- The United Nations Framework Convention on Climate Change (UNFCCC)[118]

The state of the global measures on climate action is a bit of a challenge for activists like Thunberg. For example, the United Nations Framework Convention on Climate Change (UNFCCC), adopted in 1992 is a key global environmental measure, and states in relevant part that its objective is to "stabilize greenhouse gas concentrations in the atmosphere at a level that would prevent dangerous anthropogenic[119],[120] interference with the climate system." Indeed, according to scientists, human impact on the environment or anthropogenic impact on the environment includes changes to biophysical environments and ecosystems, biodiversity, and natural resources, caused directly or indirectly by humans, including global warming, environmental degradation, ocean acidification, mass extinction and biodiversity loss, ecological crisis, and ecological collapse.[121]

In essence, and especially in light of growing human population, according to scientists, human efforts of modifying our environment to fit the needs of society is causing severe effects. For example, some human activities causing global harm include, overconsumption, overexploitation, pollution, and deforestation, among others. Our harmful human practices are actually an existential threat to humanity, owing partly to the catastrophic outcomes of global warming and biodiversity loss.[122]

Some of the implementation challenges that the framework delineate include non-binding limits on greenhouse gas emissions for individual countries, and no enforcement mechanisms to hold signatories accountable. Rather, international treaties vis a vis protocols or agreements are suggested to be negotiated to specify the implementation actions to help realize the aspirations of the UNFCCC which currently has 197 parties.

A UNFCCC implementing agreement which Thunberg has brought to the world's attention is the Paris Agreement. This agreement which was adopted in 2015 governs emission reductions from 2020 onward through commitments of countries with Nationally Determined Contributions (NDCs); this is with a goal to lower the target to less than 2 °C, here, such as the 1.5 °C, preindustrial times level. What this means is that in light of the imminent harm around climate crisis, the Paris Agreement helps to set a criterion for signatories to adhere to, without which the objectives of the UNFCCC may come to fruition.

According to environmental and climate experts, the extent to which wealthier country parties will effectively implement their commitments under the UNFCCC, will impact the effective implementation of not so wealthy country parties of their commitments under the UNFCCC: specifically, those commitments related to financial contributions, and transfer of technology. Further, the progress will take fully into account the fact that economic and social development and poverty eradication are the first and overriding priorities of the not so wealthy country parties. In other words, political will and equity are key components of the successful realization of the UNFCCC and its enabling measures such as in the Paris Agreement, Kyoto Protocol, Bali Action Plan, the Copenhagen Accord, the Cancún Agreements and the Durban Platform for Enhanced Action, among others.[123]

The message is clear: destabilizing the climate adversely impacts vulnerable people in derogation of the United Nations' commitment to "leave no one behind" as espoused in various environmental agreements, and the Sustainable Development Goals (SDGs).

According to Thunberg during her Madrid UN Climate Conference speech, "the world is running on empty" possibly on fumes, as we are rapidly squandering our declining carbon budgets through our anthropogenic action of contributing to escalated global warming.[124] Additionally, in many of her presentations, she cites the Intergovernmental Panel on

Climate Change's Special Report on Global Warming of 1.5 °C, (SR 1.5 IPCC), which is the guiding document on achieving the objectives outlined in the Paris Agreement.

She debunks the notion that future generations possess the resources to assume and tackle hundreds of billions of tons of CO2 the air is already polluted with through transcendental and supernatural technologies that have yet to be invented. She admonishes that the keyway towards solutions is by rolling up our sleeves and investing the hard work and resources. As a global family, "we indeed have some work to do but some more than others" Thunberg warns us.[125]

Some of the stumbling blocks around progress include when countries evade their responsibilities by not keeping their word, by double counting and moving their emissions-causing further damage to less wealthy countries.[126]

Thus, just like the brilliant civil rights community organizing of everyday people by the great Baker, part of Thunberg's strategy is making every day people aware of the existential threat of global warming, so that they are empowered to put pressure on their political leaders, because "without pressure from the people, our leaders can get away with basically not doing anything, which is where we are now."[127] The COVID-19 pandemic is a sombre reminder of what could happen in a world that is apathetic towards an existential threat through inaction. My fear is that there could be catastrophic impediments to all humans if there was a planetary environmental crisis.

However, I am encouraged by Thunberg's words that she remains hopeful in the recent developments that the "people who have been unaware…are now starting to wake up. And in fact, every great change throughout history has come from the people. We do not have to wait.

We can start the change right now. We, the people."[128] Thunberg's activism and seat at the table reminds us of the hardest to reach, who have limited access - women and girls who are the most impacted by climate crises and planetary dangers, thus holding our feet to the fire for our own good and for the future of generations yet unborn.

Women's Movements and Violence
TIME'S UP Legal Defense Fund

According to the United Nations, 1 in 5 women and girls, including 19 percent of women and girls aged 15 to 49, have experienced physical and/ or sexual violence over a 12 month period. Yet, 49 countries have no laws that specifically protect women from such violence.[129]

In 2018, as part of the response to the mounting sexual assault allegations against a well-known film producer, and the groundswell of mobilization around the #MeToo campaign, Hollywood celebrities launched the TIME'S UP Legal Defense Fund (TULDF), raising over $20 million.[130]

It is a legal defense fund administered by the National Women's Law Center Fund LLC,[131] with a mandate of fighting against sexual harassment and assault. It is noteworthy that Justice Ruth Bader Ginsburg began her career within the women's movement in a similar initiative, which she helped spearhead at the American Civil Liberties Union, here, the "Women's Law Project," an impact litigation, and public interest law focused initiative, known for advancing the rights of women and girls.[132]

Los Angeles, USA. 14th January, 2018: A general view of atmosphere of Times Up billboard on Sunset Blvd in Los Angeles, California. Credit: Barry King

The organizers of the TIME'S UP Legal Defense Fund mobilized over 700 pro bono lawyers, advocated for legislation to punish companies that tolerate persistent harassment, and continue to work towards gender parity in Hollywood and within low wage service professions where women often dominate. The initiative also encourages women to continue to speak truth to justice by empowering and training them. The organisation's President is Tina Tchen, Former Executive Director of the White House Council on Women and Girls, and Former Chief of Staff to First Lady Michelle Obama. [133]

This movement emphasizes the powerful role of the media, entertainment industry, civil society and non-traditional state actors in mobilizing visibility and resources for peace and security. It also highlights, the critical role of the legal profession, through impact litigation to positively effect policies. Additionally, it underscores the necessary role of media, public relations institutions, and the various pressure points that can impact public and private institutional policy change for gender protection, empowerment and mainstreaming.

A notable TULDF achievement was the "Silence Breakers" initiative via various social media platforms including Twitter, providing a seat at the table for survivors of sexual assault to have their voices heard and inspire others to speak truth to justice. The "Silence Breakers" were honored as Time Magazine's Person of the Year.[134]

The TULDF prioritizes cases involving at risk populations including: low-wage workers, people of color, LGBTQ people, individuals with disabilities, those facing retaliation because they dared to speak out, among other groups. They also provide targeted support for women in male-dominated occupations, workers facing harassment or threats by especially high profile individuals, multiple individuals within one workplace, novel or precedent-setting areas in the law, and extreme retaliation against those alleging harassment.[135] The TULDF protects survivors through various strategies including lawsuits or media campaigns. The TULDF acquires safety, equity, and power for women while they earn their livelihood. The fund also conducts know your rights campaign training that empower women at the workplace, upholding the notion that every woman deserves to feel safe and respected at work and fight to make that vision a reality.[136]

According to its 2019 factsheet, the TULDF received 4,335 requests for assistance in 50 U.S. states related to workplace sexual assault and or harassment. Additionally, the TULDF provides outreach grants to organizations that work with low-wage workers, immigrant workers, and other marginalized groups. They focus on workers who may feel they do not have a voice at their workplace, by providing educational training and information about workplace sexual harassment; these efforts have created a support system that could motivate them to come forward or support a colleague who has spoken truth to justice.

The TULDF and the women discussed in the manifesto embody the late Maya Angelou's poem "Still I Rise" where women and girls continue to rise to the occasion, rise to make their world a better place even though they had to face challenges that sought to break their spirits, souls, and bodies. The truth of the matter is that it does take a village and time to unravel the vestiges of inequality towards women and girls. We still have a long way to go, but we cannot let the fight ahead scare us, for the battle is always God's, but yet we must meet God halfway like angels on earth - fighting like it depends only on us, but trusting like it depends on God, which ultimately it does.

The TULDF story inspires us to believe that among other classifications, gender, wealth, power and immigration status, do not have to be a stumbling block to women defending their personhood; we can and should reject our objectification in society. Indeed, TULDF occupies an important civil society space for women and girls, much like their predecessors, which include the Civil Rights and Labor movements and other initiatives within the women's movement such as the #Metoo campaign. There are many other notable organizations that have advanced principles of women's empowerment including the: Women of Color Advancing Peace, Security and Conflict Transformation (WCAPS), spearheaded by Ambassador Bonnie Jenkins, creating a seat for hundreds of women across the globe from the Americas to Europe to Africa and everywhere in between; Women and Girls Africa Summit (WAGS), CODEPINK, and Women for Peace, Leadership Council for Women in National Security (LCWINS), among others. As the TULDF has successfully brought powerful men to justice, we are reminded of the importance of economic empowerment, resource mobilization, and community organizing, to advance the efforts of civil society, particularly as relates to the peace and security of women and girls.

The main objectives of this manifesto are not only to inspire women and girls, but to also get us thinking, and hopefully wholesomely catalyse a reckoning and honest discourse on the importance of hedging the movement for women's empowerment! This includes securing protections from the evils of political convenience, moral distractions, micro aggression and personal agendas that call into question and undermine good work that is being carried out. It makes no sense for us to take two steps forward, and then four steps backwards.

Indeed, much like Yousafzai's and Thunberg's efforts, the stories shared by sexual assault survivors compelled the global community to pay attention from Rome, Italy, to Durban, South Africa, to Oakland, California and everywhere in between, and the accused became household names, but not for good reason. For a lot of women, girls, men, and boys, the accused embodied the predatory impact of power and privilege unchecked, wreaking sexual atrocities and creating an insecure society for their survivors and society, corrupting the human moral compass.

Fortunately, their time was up; the golden hour and social contract of combatting sexual assault allowed women to be present at this table through the TULDF's visibility efforts complementing the ongoing legal cases. Indeed, women of all walks, persuasions, and statuses were empowered and publicly came forward offering their testimony, building the body of evidence to substantiate a compelling case of a history of sexual violence and predatory behaviour.

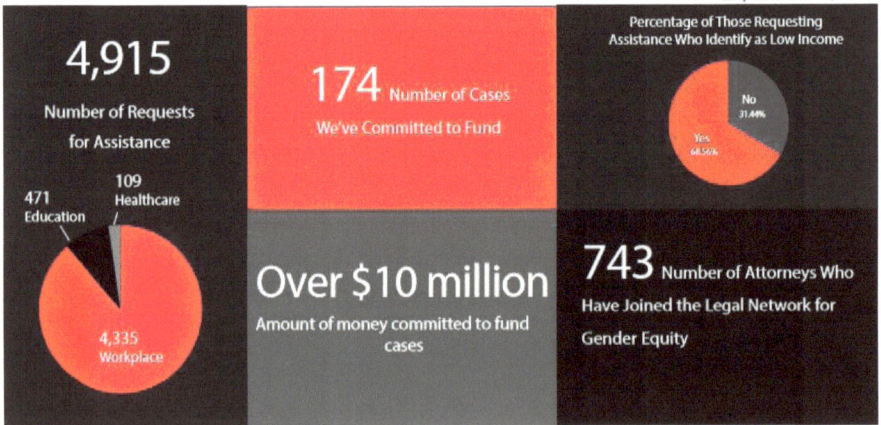

TIME'S UP
LEGAL DEFENSE FUND

The TIME'S UP Legal Defense Fund, administered by the National Women's Law Center Fund, is a groundbreaking initiative that connects those who experience workplace sexual harassment and related retaliation with legal and media assistance. The Fund connects workers seeking assistance with its network of attorneys. The Fund helps defray the costs of selected legal cases especially for low-wage workers; women in male-dominated occupations; workers who are facing defamation suits; and workers who are fired or blacklisted after reporting harassment.

Last Updated on November 18, 2019

4,915
Number of Requests for Assistance

471 Education
109 Healthcare
4,335 Workplace

174 Number of Cases We've Committed to Fund

Over $10 million
Amount of money committed to fund cases

Percentage of Those Requesting Assistance Who Identify as Low Income
No 31.44%
Yes 68.56%

743 Number of Attorneys Who Have Joined the Legal Network for Gender Equity

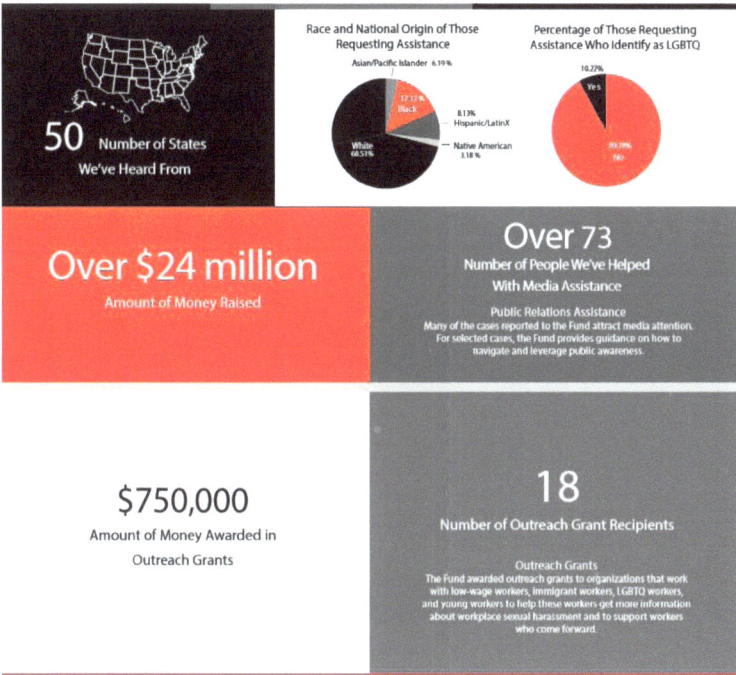

In the end the accused were ostracized from the same institutions they once ruled over, including termination from major companies, and expulsion from notable professional organizations.

Moreover, in addition to criminal convictions in the United States, other legal battles continue to mount abroad. In the U.S., a particular case was furthered via a civil class action lawsuit in New York, which case also calls into question the moral compass, accountability and complicity of some companies who had done business with the accused. This is evidence that the private sector also has a key role to play in the protection of women and girls, and that the failure to do so will not only tarnish a company's image, but could also substantially impact its bottom line. Respect for the rule of law in the private sector is a wise practice.

Additionally, in Hollywood, the Los Angeles County District Attorney's Office's special sexual assault task force was created to address these types of criminal conduct issues. So, the tides of change are moving this evolving movement towards its becoming, which is hopefully towards justice.

All efforts taken by all the women, girls and movements in this manifesto reinforce one another, anchoring the importance of the rights of women and girls. But what about enforcement mechanisms? Some of the critiques around women's rights efforts have discussed the laws on the books not necessarily ensuring justice. Are these laws being enforced, and if so by who? The role of civil society groups within the women's movement has proven to be critical to enforcing the laws on the books; they also have the ability to impact litigation, setting the precedents that would help move the needle towards change.

Movements are Important

Since movements are important to spur systemic change, the TULDF has positioned itself to occupy an important seat at the table and an opportune space: a unique role as an independent entity, unencumbered by politics and or profit. It has the opportunity to uphold the rule of law and shatter the ecosystem of sexual assault across the value chain.

The TULDF ought to be navigated by the mandate that the organization is not trying to mobilize a political base or make money for shareholders. It is important for the TULDF to unequivocally take the stance that survivors are their base and their shareholders. A curious inquiry that I have pondered is what is the magnitude of the TULDF's geographic scope? Will it be limited to the U.S., or expand to remote parts of the globe - building the local capacity of advocates and media who can represent women and girls in dire need? Can the TULDF champion issues and spark movements on issues in the global south, for instance primary school girls or university students forced to exchange sex for grades on the continent of Africa or Civil Servants, private sector and Nollywood women faced with a daily barrage of sexual assault at the work place in the continent?

The TULDF is eliminating the boundaries and expanding the resources available to women to fight violence, by creating a fund that not only works to bring justice to survivors of sexual violence and harassment, but eliminates a major barrier: the financial and human resources needed to secure legal counsel in such matters! They create an ecosystem of community support, upon whose shoulders survivors can stand - even as they struggle to retell and relive horrendous injustices against their personhood, peace, and security. Most importantly, the TULDF takes the shame away from the survivors, surrounding them with a community that is actively rallying and working to make sure their voice is being heard; it empowers survivors who may be in hiding, informing them that the time is now to tell their story, allowing them to commence their journey towards healing; it reinforces that the time is up for the perpetrators. Underrepresented women in the workplace are encouraged to "lean in," and take a seat at the table while would be predators are put on notice that the vanguards and watchdogs with TULDF (and other important stakeholders in the women's movement), are slowly but surely chipping away at the institutions and policies that perpetuate and foster insecurity for women and girls in achieving self-determination.

In this "golden hour" the TULDF is bringing about change by shining light on sexual violence, inspired by #MeToo and other initiatives, captivating our imagination in the fight for peace and security for women and girls, delivered to the masses in real time, thanks to the power of social media!

Nobel Peace Prize Nominee: Black Lives Matter

BET Black Girls Rock! 2016 at New Jersey Performing Arts Center - Show Featuring: Alicia Garza, Opall Tometi.Newark, New Jersey, United States.01 Apr 2016. Contributor: WENN Rights Ltd

There is power in words.

When it comes to the peace and security of women and girls, language matters. From TIME'S UP to #MeToo, to Si Se Puede!… all of these declarative statements set the tone and tenure for the gains that they seek.

Therefore, the work of Black Lives Matter (BLM) is so important for global racial equality. Singlehandedly, the BLM movement embodies how when women take a seat at the table, they can achieve four key objectives: 1) question the status quo; 2) set a movement for change in motion; 3) set policy change in motion; and 4) serve as the watchdogs of effective change implementation. BLM through its global and local community organizing and power sharing is redefining what it means to end systemic racism globally, and what it means to be a Black woman in today's world.

On July 13, 2013, Alicia Garza, Patrisse Cullors and Opal Tometi, three African American women and community organizers articulated the #BlackLivesMatter movement. It was in response to the acquittal of a vigilante who murdered 17-year-old Trayvon Benjamin Martin, a Black American teenager in Florida. Since inception, the movement's mission has been to eradicate white supremacy and to build member led local power to intervene in violence inflicted on Black communities by the state, and vigilantes - such as the one who murdered 17-year-old Martin.

By combating and countering acts of violence, creating space for Black imagination and innovation, and centering Black joy, BLM actively realizes justice for Black communities. According to the organization, it remains committed to struggling together, imagining and creating a world free of anti-Blackness, where every Black person has the social, economic, and political power to thrive. BLM's stated intention is to connect Black people from all over the world who have a shared desire for justice to act together in their communities. Indeed, the organization's leaders articulate that they are unapologetically Black in their positioning. They assert that "in affirming that Black Lives Matter, we need not qualify our position. To love and desire freedom and justice for ourselves is a prerequisite for wanting the same for others. We see ourselves as part of the global Black family, and we are aware of the different ways we are impacted or privileged as Black people who exist in different parts of the world…we embody and practice justice, liberation, and peace in our engagements with one another."[137]

Specifically, BLM inspires us to believe that race, gender, systemic racism, modern day Jim Crow laws, and police brutality, though they may be stumbling blocks, will not prevent systemic change where there is a mobilization of global political will from all quarters of life across all races, classes and political leanings.

Self-Care

The issue that BLM champions, and which resonates, is their use of words to state the obvious but often ignored fact of black lives mattering; and indeed, the psychological impact of this linguistic exercise on the global society is striking. Words are powerful, and are at the very essence of the human experience. For instance, when we hear the words "education" "taxation" "rape" "domestic violence" "climate change" "criminal justice reform" "colonialism" "slavery" "Constitution" "human rights" and "civil rights" certain images are conjured in our hearts and minds, for better or worse. Words affirm who we are in whatever context we find ourselves. Words are a form of self-care when used positively because they nurture, encourage and spark human hope and resilience.[138]

This is why the words Black Lives Matter are so powerful. The words positively soothe, nurture, justify, humanize, give hope, empower, validate and create a seat at the table for those with whom the words resonate, regardless of their racial background, class or political beliefs.

It is consequential that BLM, through its very existence champions self-care within the Black community, because a race which is constantly on defense, will struggle to thrive, without taking time to heal/rejuvenate/care for its people. The concept of self-care through love and affirmation is one that often is considered to be a luxury in black communities across the globe; this is in part because of the history of oppression, which leaves little to no room for self-care.

However, given the amount of trauma that has been wrought upon persons of African descent, an essential element of healing from colonialism, slavery or other forms of injustice is self-care, where Black people not only survive but are given a seat at the table to thrive and contribute positively to society.

London, UK. 9 July 2016. Local residents hold a "Black Lives Matter" rally in Brixton, to show solidarity with those who lost their lives in recent police related incidents in the USA. Credit: Stephen Chung

Breathe Act

An equally important issue that BLM marshals is that of proposing tangible and actionable policy change. A prime example is the proposed "Breathe Act,"[139] named in honor of the late Eric Garner, George Floyd, Breonna Taylor, and thousands of others who have died at the hands of law enforcement. Eric Garner was a Black American man whose life was snuffed out by police officers who restrained him while he pleaded for his life; he stated over ten times that he could not breathe, until he succumbed to his lack of breath.

U.S. House Speaker Nancy Pelosi (D-CA), Senate Minority Leader Chuck Schumer (D-NY) and House Majority Leader Steny Hoyer (D-MD) kneel with Congressional Democrats during a moment of silence to honor George Floyd, Breonna Taylor, Ahmaud Arbery and others inside Emancipation Hall after weeks of protests against racial inequality in the aftermath in Minneapolis police custody of Floyd, at the U.S. Capitol in Washington, U.S., June 8, 2020. REUTERS/ Jonathan Ernst TPX IMAGES OF THE DAY

Through his words, Garner stated the obvious: that he could not breathe. Yet his words and pleas were ignored.

With the use of social media, we were all a global witness to another black man's life being taken – George Floyd, who took his last breath, as an officer kneeled on his neck. There was also the case of 26-year-old Breonna Taylor, a Black emergency room technician who died from 6 of the 32 shots fired at her apartment during a botched police raid. Taylor received no medical attention for more than 20 minutes after she was struck.[140]

Among other objectives, the Breathe Act would eliminate federal programs and agencies that finance and expand the abusive aspects of the U.S. criminal justice and legal system and invest more in community based peace, security and public safety initiatives for all people.

Watch and Listen

Since the movement's conception, its strategy is a David and Goliath approach, using its community organizing to influence national and local policies and politics that impact the everyday lives of Black people.

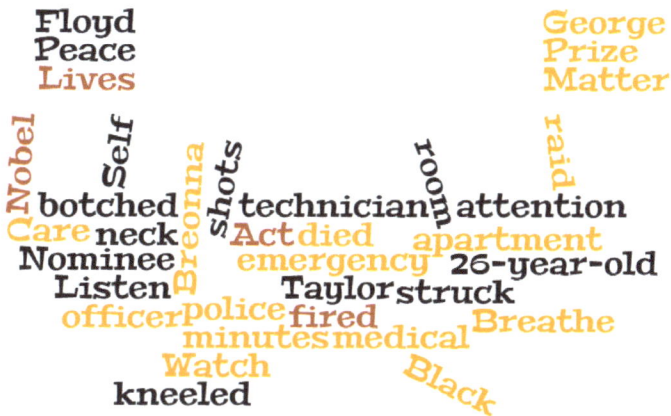

For example, BLM played a role in U.S. Presidential campaigns by challenging candidates and elected officials who were up for re-election; they demanded accountability by requiring them to recognize the humanity of persons of African descent. In 2020, BLM challenged then Presidential candidate, and Mayor of South Bend, Indiana Peter Buttigieg for his perceived lack of understanding the plight of his African American constituents.[141] Through BLM's WhatMatters2020, community members continue to be mobilized, and be inspired to be more civically engaged, by registering to vote, voting, turning people out to vote, and donating to candidates who have committed to carrying out the Black agenda.[142]

On the local level, BLM tackle issues that impact local livelihoods, and pose as an affront to the local peace and security. For example, their police accountability, expungement series, and driver's license renewal program are all geared towards addressing intersecting traumas caused by intersecting exposures to domination, and the imperative to provide restorative justice to community members.[143]

Like many activists before them, BLM has been deemed by some as being a radical group, with violent propensity. However, as a trained lawyer, I observe the facts that I can verify as at the publication of this manifesto. In reviewing the body of evidence, facts, and the tangible results from the legislative measures - to the policy documents - to their engagement and education of elected officials on the plight of persons of African descent: their achievements are quite impressive for a movement. Indeed, according to the founders, Black Lives Matter is a woman created ideological and political intervention in a world where Black lives are systematically and intentionally targeted for demise. [The movement] is an affirmation of Black folks' humanity, [their] contributions to this society, and [their] resilience in the face of deadly oppression. BLM [are organizers and community] members [who both] see and understand the significant gaps in movement spaces and leadership.[144] Black Lives Matter's Global Network infrastructure is adaptive and decentralized, with a set of guiding principles. [The organization consistently] supports the development of new Black leaders, as well as creates a [ever-expanding] network, through which Black people feel empowered to determine [their] destinies in [their] communities.

Louisville, Kentucky, USA. 25th Sep, 2020. Children and their moms talk about the Breonna Taylor memorial as protestors get ready for the march for Justice. Credit: Amy Katz

The BLM Network credit ordinary people from St. Louis and Ferguson, Missouri, who put their bodies on the line day in and day out and show up for Black lives.[145] Indeed, as the world reckons with the shame of colonialism, slavery and the vestiges of these institutions of injustice, we need the BLM ladies seating at the table as the watchdogs against further injustices that can result from global systemic racism. We ought to be heartened that they will continue to serve as the conscience of the world. We ought to be grateful that they serve as our unapologetic North Star in this regard.

For All the People: U.S. Vice President Kamala Harris

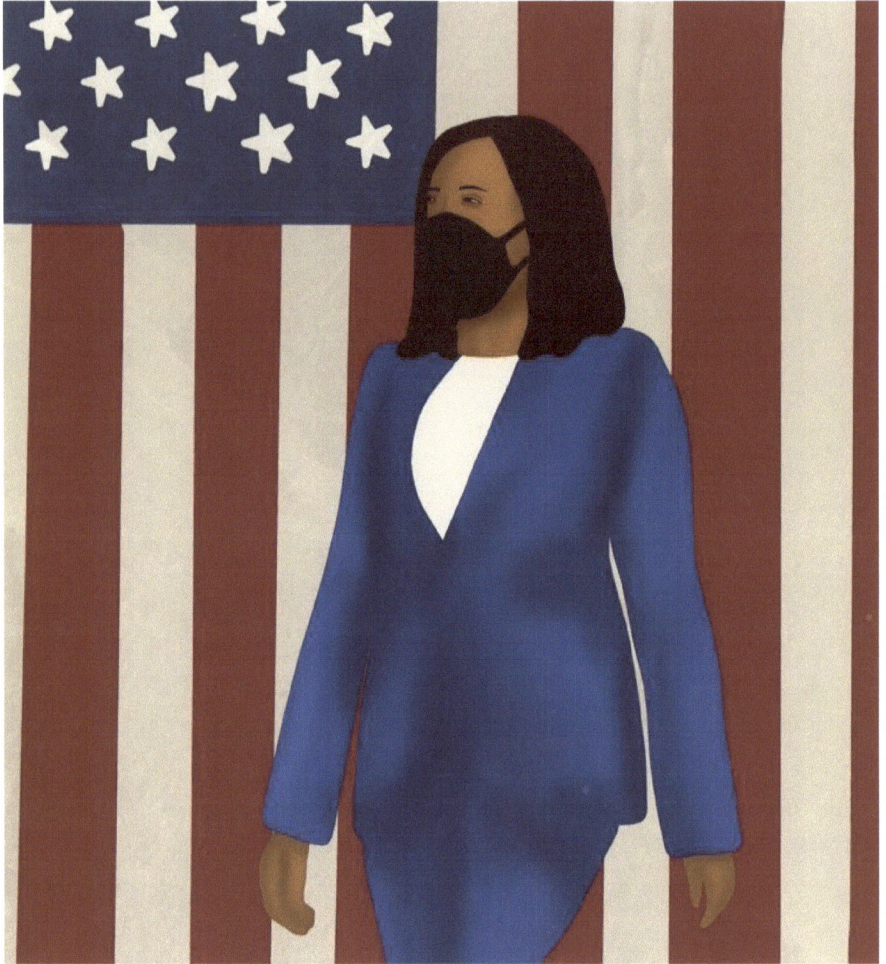

U.S. Vice President Kamala Harris. Illustration by Sarah Dahir (SOUTH AFRICA)

Like some of the BLM founders, Kamala Harris makes me and other Oaklanders extremely proud!

Born on October 20, 1964, at Kaiser hospital in Oakland, California, U.S. Vice-President Kamala Harris is my former boss, and she is the epitome of the different seats women and girls can have at the table at different times in their lives. Harris has taken on numerous leadership seats throughout her career.[146]

Some of the seats she has held include: President of her law school's National Black Law Students Association, Deputy District Attorney in Alameda County, California, and many other seats in between, before she became the first person of color elected as the District Attorney of San Francisco. She has held many more seats before being elected Vice President of the United States.[147]

Harris demonstrates that we do not have to remain static in our seat at the table. For some, moving from seat to seat enables them to use their different talents. For some, staying in the same seat gives them the steady hand to push for resilient change like Speaker of the U.S. House of Representatives Nancy Pelosi.

In the case of Chief Olufunmilayo Ransome Kuti, she moved from educator to negotiator, to community organizer and community leader— occupying different seats at the different tables in her life. Similarly, Supreme Court Justice Ruth Bader Ginsburg held the seats of law professor and women's rights litigator, until she took her final seat on the U.S. Supreme Court bench. Finally, with Dr. Condoleezza Rice, her seats included: Provost at Stanford University, National Security Advisor, U.S. Secretary of State, and later as thought leader for the Hoover Institution at Stanford University.

From the head seat to the corner seat and everywhere in between, what has made the women in this manifesto so compelling is their ability to confidently create a seat for, or pull up a chair for other women and girls. I am proud to say that Vice President Harris created a seat for me and others. Indeed, I do not take this legacy for granted, and I will try my best to continue to pay it forward.

I had the pleasure of working for her when she served as the District Attorney of the City and County of San Francisco, California (DA's office). Like the women highlighted in this manifesto, she was the first in many roles that she took on. Then, she was the first Black and South Asian American woman to serve as District Attorney. She then went on to serve as the first African American and South Asian American woman Attorney General in California.[148] She continues to make history as the first woman, first Black, and first South-Asian American, elected to the Vice Presidency.[149]

President Joe Biden and Vice President Kamala Harris meet with Secretary of State Antony Blinken Thursday, Feb. 4, 2021, at the U.S. State Department in Washington, D.C. (Official White House Photo by Adam Schultz)

In her capacity as Vice President, she occupies the powerful seat as the President of the U.S. Senate; serving as the deciding tie-breaker vote to pass legislation in the U.S. Congress before it goes to the President for his signature into law.

At the DA's office, I was a bright eyed first year law student with clarity on what I wanted to be—an international lawyer. However, I was counseled by a mentor to become a leader in the National Black Law Students Association, which I did. I was also counseled to pursue work as a certified law clerk at the prestigious San Francisco DA's office—a position that a lot of law students coveted. I was advised that the writing and speaking experiences that I would get would be unlike any other, because the office nurtured, groomed, and provided great opportunities for the law clerks to grow as public servants. I took the good advice bestowed upon me and split my summer. I spent the first half at DA Harris' office, where among other duties, I was entrusted with the opportunities to work with Assistant District Attorneys and investigators, draft various motions, and attend numerous preliminary hearings, including conducting a hearing. I was also one of the lucky ones to get to sit in on high profile prosecutions, including one where the DA had to come in to argue the matter. It was a very intense summer of learning, making connections, and seeing what women are capable of accomplishing. From my direct supervisors, both of whom were women, all the way up to our big boss DA Harris — to the judges in the courtrooms, the court support staff, and so on— seeing so many women in leadership seats was a humbling and inspiring experience. As a young lawyer in training, everywhere around me there was a reinforcement to my psyche that women—when given the platform and a seat at the table, were not only capable, but often exceeded the call of duty.

On top of all of that, one morning as I arrived at the Hall of Justice in San Francisco and hopped onto the elevator, to my surprise, the DA herself hopped on with me! As I tried to excuse myself so that she could ride alone (out of respect), she stopped me and flashed me that warm smile of hers. She asked about me, how I was enjoying the clerkship, and encouraged me to keep up the good work. Just as I was thanking her for the opportunity the elevator reached her floor, and she said her goodbye. That was one of the highlights of my clerkship, because it exposed me to the authenticity of now Vice President Harris. Even though I was keenly aware that she was busy, that was not conveyed in our interaction. Like my encounters with RBG and Rice, reflecting upon my elevator experience with Harris, I was reminded again of the saying that although you may not remember what someone says to you, you will certainly remember the way they made you feel. That day at the Hall of Justice she made me feel I could achieve anything. I took note of this, and try to emulate this attractive trait to my utmost ability.

Harris attributes her inspiration to her mother who was an Indian-American immigrant, activist, and breast cancer researcher. Harris' trajectory and attraction to justice is embodied in her life's work for "the people," as her Presidential campaign slogan "Kamala Harris for the People" declared.

Harris worked her way up the ranks as a public servant and the people's lawyer; it is therefore not surprising that she continues to serve the American people in the second highest office in the land. She utilized her prosecutorial discretion to show mercy and grant grace. For example, she started a program that enabled first-time drug offenders the chance to earn a high school diploma and find employment. This work inspired me and aligned with my prior work at the Ella Baker Center for Human Rights "Books Not Bars" initiative in Oakland, California.

As the first Black woman to serve two terms as Attorney General, Harris won a historical $25 billion settlement for California homeowners hit by the foreclosure crisis that adversely impacted communities of color in the Bay Area and across the country. She also supported California's landmark climate change law, protected the Affordable Care Act, and was instrumental in the prosecution of transnational gangs that trafficked in guns, drugs, and human beings.[150]

Harris' 2017 swearing in as a United States Senator for California made her the second Black American woman, and first South Asian-American senator in U.S. history. The world was able to view her prosecutorial prowess during hearings when she was on the powerful Senate Judiciary Committee. One of her most notable moments, in my opinion, was when she interrogated a Supreme Court Justice nominee accused of sexual violence against women. Harris asked a combination of targeted and broader policy questions about the nominee's prior lower court rulings. She asked about his views on a woman's right to choose, the presence of racial discrimination in various sectors, and the implications of his views on Section 5 of the Voting Rights Act during the confirmation hearing. Harris showed the world her commitment to advocate for fair judges who will decide on policy issues that affect the well-being of everyday people, with an eye towards building an inclusive America that empowers all, regardless of their status in life.[151]

While serving as a Senator, Harris fought to raise wages for working people, reform the U.S. criminal justice system by addressing the broader issue of systemic racism, helped to make healthcare a right for all Americans, tackled the epidemic of substance abuse, and worked towards expanding access to childcare for working parents.

With the remaining half of my summer after I completed my DA clerkship, I travelled to Oxford, England to study international human rights and humanitarian law with some of the world's renowned experts in the field, many of whom were women. With all the exposure to women leaders in the legal field from my summer experiences, it became the norm for me to see women sitting at the table as leaders. This encouraged me to vie for and be appointed as the Executive Director of the National Black Students Association, Western Region. Later on as a young lawyer, I was appointed as the Chairwoman of the American Bar Association Young Lawyers Division, International Law Committee, where my team and I grew the committee's membership from under 70 members to over 400 members during my tenure through programs and publications.

To be frank, these were not opportunities that I would have sought out on my own. I am so fortunate for having experienced so much exposure to women leaders. These engagements helped me to form my professional personality. Oftentimes, women empower and inspire others, even though they may not realize it, just by virtue of being at the table. This brings to mind Congresswoman Sheila Jackson Lee of Texas, a formidable and powerful U.S. senior legislator, known for her no-nonsense personality and the first woman ranking member of the House Judiciary Subcommittee on Crime, Terrorism, Homeland Security, and Investigations.

She hired me as her foreign affairs staffer. She trusted my work, and gave me wings to fly. We drafted and introduced numerous legislative measures on the global rights of women and girls and persons of African descent. Indeed, one of our Capitol Hill Congressional Briefing Series on UNSCR 1325 on Women, Peace and Security earned the Member of Congress the Charles T. Manatt Democracy Award, in Washington, DC.

I remember one of my first assignments for the Congresswoman was as her plus one when President Ashraf Ghani of the Islamic Republic of Afghanistan addressed a Joint Meeting of Congress, where he articulated his continued vision for peace building in his homeland.

My very last assignment with her was at the German Marshall Fund of the United States, where she was one of the speakers at an event entitled

"Advancing Women of Color in Transatlantic Leadership." The initiative convened guests and speakers to discuss the development of an inter-generational leadership pipeline to foster support and community among women of color from senior leaders to rising talent. That afternoon, the Congresswoman delivered one of her inspiring speeches of empowerment to the over 65 women convened. She also belabored my pending departure to the UN in Rome, Italy, but tempered it with her blessing during her remarks.

Women in the labor movement have also been instrumental in nourishing my professional DNA, providing me a seat at the table. President Alice Goff, Executive Director Cheryl Parisi, Organizing and Legal Director Leslie Simon, and Political Coordinator Dolores Spears, formerly of the American Federation of State County and Municipal Employees (AFSCME) District Council 36 poured so much into me when they mentored me as a young labor lawyer and organizer. Los Angeles weather was beautiful, but so were the experiences I had with the women labor leaders. In the very early part of my career, they provided me numerous seats at the table where I negotiated on behalf of, organized, and represented working people. Like the Congresswoman, they trusted my work and fortified my abilities with resources that enabled my growth and independence. A lot of the values they instilled in me remain in my professional DNA and have stood me in good stead at various tables.

People often teased me and asked whether or not I would work for Harris, either as her staffer when she was a Senator or during the administration in her role as U.S. Vice President. I always responded that I don't know. What I do know for sure, is that my exposure to her achievements have propelled me to achieve more than I ever imagined, and it has motivated me to pay it forward. If the sole purpose for our life paths crossing is to inspire me that sky is the limit, then this is a cause for celebration from my vantage point. I remain a proud supporter and cheerleader for Harris, for not only paving the way, but also opening the door and providing seats for me and other women at the table—during the golden hours of our careers.

I attended a rally in my hometown of Oakland, California where then Senator Harris rolled out her campaign "Kamala for the People." I was visiting from Rome, Italy on holiday from my assignment with the UN. My family beamed with pride to see one of Oakland's finest and brightest shine on the national and world stage. After the rally, we treated ourselves to a yummy meal at our local small business favourite restaurant, Lake Chalet near Lake Merritt, while enjoying the jazz music playing outside. I kept my campaign placard as a souvenir of history-little did I know more history would be made!

Fast forward to August 2020, after spirited Democratic Presidential debates, Joe Biden, the presumptive Democratic Presidential candidate picked Harris as his running mate.[152] This made Harris, who has been the first in so many roles, the first African American woman and the first person of South-Asian descent to be nominated for national office by a major party and only the fourth woman in U.S. history to be chosen for a presidential ticket.

Vice President Harris inspires us to believe that we can also be the first in unchartered territory. Race and gender are surmountable barriers for women and girls who seek a seat at the table and to bring others along. Her election on the 100th anniversary of the 19th Amendment of the U.S. Constitution, is a testament to the importance of voting and an encouraging sign that there is progress towards equity, equality, and empowerment for women and girls.

Beijing + 25, UN Sustainable Development Goal 5, and UNSCR 1325

New York, UN headquarters in New York. 13th Oct, 2015. UN Women chief Phumzile Mlambo-Ngcuka addresses the Security Council during a meeting on "Women, peace and security" at the UN headquarters in New York, Oct. 13, 2015. United Nations Security Council on Tuesday adopted a resolution to further strenghen women's role in peace and security, 15 years after the adoption of the landmark resolution 1325. Credit: Li Muzi/Xinhua

2020 was a challenging year for everyone. Lost loved ones, lost savings, lost livelihoods, and weakened human rights. It has also been a seminal year in the continuous history of women's rights. The 19th Amendment of the U.S. Constitution turned 100. We saw the global community mark the 25th anniversary of the Fourth World Conference on Women and the adoption of the Beijing Declaration and Platform for Action (1995). Beijing+25 is a visionary agenda for the empowerment of women and girls, whereby 189 governments committed to address global issues that were unprecedented in scope. The agenda covers 12 important social policy issues, all of which this manifesto addresses: poverty, education and training, health, violence, armed conflict, economy, power and decision-making, institutional mechanisms, human rights, media, environment, and the girl child.[153]

It was also at the Fourth World Conference on Women that Presidential candidate Hillary Clinton declared women's rights as human rights.

Governments, civil society, and other stakeholders committed to work towards eliminating discrimination against women and girls; with a goal to achieve equality in all quarters of life whether in public or private spaces. Some of the stated objectives of Beijing+25 include removal of discriminatory laws, combatting all forms of violence against women and girls including harmful practices, investing in and educating girls, economic empowerment of women through access to employment and other opportunities, women's participation and representation in national and local politics and policy making, and the imperative of advancing joint efforts to ensure peace and security for women and girls globally.

According to UN Women Executive Director, Dr. Phumzile Mlambo-Ngcuka, although much has been achieved, progress has been slow and uneven, particularly for the most marginalized women and girls who experience multiple intersecting forms of discrimination. It is heart-breaking that their challenging situations have been exacerbated by COVID-19; this pandemic has exposed and worsened existing limitations to access to opportunities for women and girls.[154]

This was part of Mlambo-Ngcuka's message to my former boss Congresswoman Sheila Jackson Lee. During her visit to Capitol Hill, Mlambo-Ngcuka underscored the importance of the UN Sustainable

Development Goal 5 on gender equality. She stated that achieving this goal is at the core of a peaceful, prosperous, and sustainable world.[155] The part of her talking points which resonated the most with my boss and others, was her prior work and efforts to empower women and girls as the first woman Deputy President of South Africa, Member of Parliament, Deputy Minister in the Department of Trade and Industry, Minister of Minerals and Energy, and acting Minister of Arts, Culture, Science and Technology.

Like Beijing+25, another seminal celebration in 2020 was the UN Security Council Resolution 1325 on women, peace, and security turning 20. This subject matter has become more relevant in the age of COVID-19, where marginalized women and girls are in even more danger due to the access issues that the pandemic poses. COVID-19 is a sober reminder of the importance of placing the role of women within the context of war and peace—the centerpiece for achieving progress. When I think of 1325, I remember traveling on a mission as a staffer with the UN World Food Programme. We traveled to northeastern Nigeria to increase visibility around the challenges that the people we served faced in the most remote parts of the world. A substantial part of my visit included visiting refugee camps, health centers, and general food distribution centers. I interacted with internally displaced women and children; these women, who were fleeing from violence, stood in line to get their monthly food ration and or health checks for them and their babies.

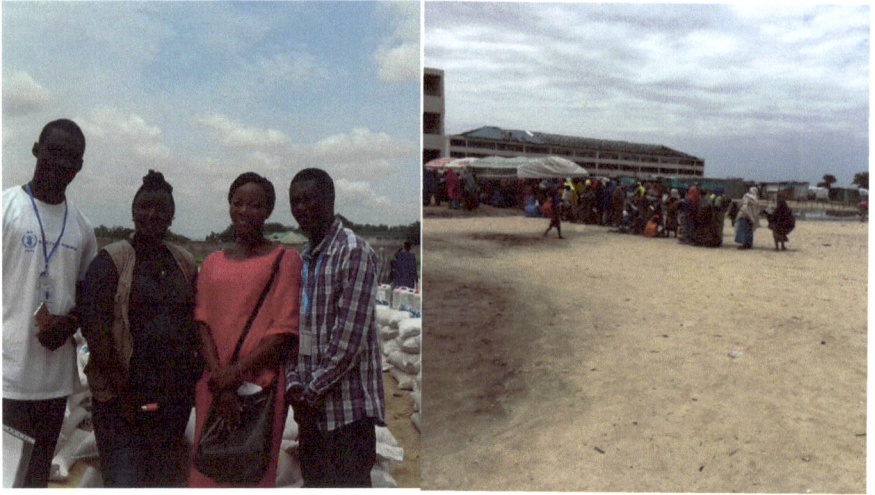

Me and field colleagues in Maiduguri, Northeastern Nigeria (L); Internally Displaced Persons (IDPs) women in line for their monthly foodbasket (R). July 2017. Credit Abiola Afolayan

Typically, when people think of security concerns, they think of non-state actors who are carrying out violent attacks. However, my field visit exposed me to another group which I observed as a threat to peace and security for these often-unaccompanied displaced women and girls: the local security forces. I vividly recall them being all male, and quite aggressive towards the women who had been displaced by Boko Haram. They were carrying militarized weaponry, and at times whipping the women with sticks. As a humanitarian worker, and someone who has worked with different law enforcement bodies, I felt fear for my life, due to the presence of the security forces who were ostensibly present to protect. As such, I can only imagine how these women felt everyday as they patiently waited in line, unsure of whether or not they would make it back alive from getting their food aid. From what I could observe, there appeared no accountability mechanisms to mitigate the visible abuse of power in this remote part of the world. For me, this was very troubling.

I could never forget those women, and I have since carried them with me. I often wondered how different the environment would have been, if the security forces were women, or if the men were better equipped to interact with the women – with compassion, as opposed to violence – as true allies of the women.

Pregnant and lactating IDP mothers in Maiduguri, Northeastern Nigeria (L); More Displaced women in line for their monthly foodbasket while security staff monitor the food (R). July 2017. Credit: Abiola Afolayan

Indeed, these are some of the issues that 1325 and other measures are meant to address, so that women and girls are not traumatized over and over, from cradle to grave - across a wide variety of experiences they are faced with - as they try to navigate their destinies in a humanitarian context.

Why Women Must Always Vote

According to the Getting to Equal Report by the World Bank Group's Women Business and the Law, women globally account for 50% of the world's population, yet constitute only 10% of the elected offices, in some parts of the world; this average is across executive, legislative, or judicial platforms, in both local state or national offices.[156] If women make up half of the world's population, why then aren't more women being elected to office? This question may be addressed by a number of factors related to cultural barriers that we identified in the case of the late Chief Mrs. Olufunmilayo Ransome Kuti; the systemic and social barriers that we identified in the case of the late Justice Ruth Bader Ginsburg; the religious and political ideology that we identified in the case of Malala; and the racial and economic barriers that we identified in the case of Black Lives Matter, and TIME'S UP Legal Defense Fund. Since time immemorial, barriers have been erected in various societies across the globe to either stifle or regress opportunities for women and girls. The good news is that this practice can be changed, and societies can exercise true leadership. The dividends are beneficial to all. Indeed, time and time again, the data shows that a society which reflects more women in leadership will deliver for everyone.[157]

Specific efforts that can move the needle include: 1) creating local and national frameworks and action plans geared at increasing political will to advance the rights of women and girls in both public and private spaces through substantial capital and infrastructure investment; 2) ensuring prioritization of the most vulnerable women and girls, through systemic changes to the structures that pose challenges; 3) fostering a culture of transparency and accountability through data gathering on gender equality - this allows citizens to constructively hold governments accountable, and support mechanisms and movements that can exert greater influence in policy decisions; 4) enlisting men and boys as feminists and gender equality champions; and 5) maximizing innovation and technological advancements that empower women and girls.

In my view, voting is as powerful a tool as economic enfranchisement and education. This is evidenced by just how long and how hard women have had to fight for this right globally. Those in the support of the status quo understood the power that women would be able to wield, as it relates to their self-determination; they therefore could only imagine a world in which they maintained this power, and held onto women's inability to vote for as long as possible. All of the aspirations espoused in Beijing + 25 can only come to fruition through elected officials who are representatives of the everyday citizens that vote them into office. When we are able to connect the dots to recognize that our access to jobs, education, safety, roads, and other social amenities are tied to the people that we put into office - and that official's ability or inability to deliver on their promises - then we can truly appreciate the gravity of voting. Voting in general, and voting our condition more specifically, gives us the opportunity to vote our moral values. If our candidate is elected, this enables us to be better positioned to facilitate change, including more seats at the table for women and girls. Voting also allows women and their allies to distribute power into the hands of more people, as opposed to holding it in the concentrated hands of a select few; those few are unlikely to have any experience with the hardships that everyday women and girls may experience across the world - from Kampala to Detroit, and beyond. We can never take for granted how one woman or one girl can change the world for the better.

Women Cross DMZ Group, May 24, 2015 : U.S. activist Gloria Steinem (8th R), Nobel Peace Prize laureates Mairead Maguire (6th R) from Northern Ireland and Leymah Gbowee (7th R) from Liberia, walk with other activists at the Imjingak Pavilion near the demilitarized zone (DMZ) separating the two Koreas, in Paju, north of Seoul, South Korea. Contributor: Aflo Co. Ltd.

As evidenced by the case of Leymah Gbowee and the Women of Liberia Mass Action for Peace,[158] women are an incredible voting bloc, and a powerful constituency when it comes to advancing the protection of women and girls. Indeed, the work of the women of Liberia was critical to bringing an end to the Second Liberian Civil War in 2003; their lobbying of the government and opposition party members, was crucial. In recognition of her leadership in the movement, Leymah, who was at that time an everyday Liberian woman, was awarded the 2011 Nobel Peace Prize for her efforts to end the war. If we look at the track record of the women and girls highlighted in this manifesto, we will see that they have been champions of tough but important issues including economic empowerment, education, political representation, education, health, security, and environmental protection; all of these are complex political issues, that elected officials across the globe discuss and vote on. These decisions are made in their respective executive, legislative, judicial offices. Since women and girls have consistently demonstrated that they have the power to determine the outcomes of these bread and butter issues through their vote and voice…why hold back?

Where We Go From Here: The New Century for Women, Girls and Movements

If you educate and empower a girl or a woman, then she has the potential to redraw a boundary - for herself or her immediate community – but most likely for both. Unfortunately, history teaches us that there are numerous philosophies, policies, and structures which actively block women and girls fully living up to their fullest potentials. This is a strategy to keep power in the hands of a few, in derogation of the fundamental principle of allowing all persons to exercise their self-determination. The truth is that the whole of society suffers when half of society is side-lined, boxed up, and prevented from gaining knowledge; this half of society is essential to solve the many social policy issues plaguing our world. Like the legendary Etta James sang in her remake, "it's a man's world, but it means nothing without a woman or a girl." And as the African proverb says "if you want to run fast run alone. If you want to run far run together."

As described in the book *Why Nations Fail: The Origins of Power and Prosperity*, historians argue that power when concentrated in the hands of a few, usually elites and specifically men tends to deprive the population of their basic and unalienable rights of life, liberty and the pursuit of happiness. I am not an elite man, so I cannot speak to the psychology of why this is. To illustrate this, the authors embark upon a historical exploration, and presentation of facts; they then juxtapose communities and nations with similarities to emphasize the impact of extractive, absolutist, and authoritarian institutions that have regressed peace, progress, and resilience; these are compared to functioning democratic institutions that tend to facilitate inclusivity, freedom of expression, innovation, peace, security stability, economic empowerment, and other successful elements which create a multiplier effect that propels nations and communities towards prosperity.[159] In the end, there is abundant evidence that when a woman or girl thrives, the world benefits. Indeed, the women featured in this manifesto help underscore this truth. So I challenge you to ponder, why does power seek to keep women and girls silent, hidden, or violated?

Keeping this truth about power in mind, a major takeaway is that knowledge is power. Educate and empower a girl – and what happens? You will witness many generations of Mulan, Funmilayo, Ruth, Ella, Condoleezza, Leymah, Zozibini, Malala, Greta, Alicia, Opal, Patrisse, Kamala, survivors, advocates, and the TIME'S UP Legal Defense Fund. Just look at what they have done and continue to do, and know that there is more where that came from. Moreover, for a prosperous society for all, the public and private sector, as well as the society at large, must continue to invest in the education and empowerment of girls, women, and movements. Indeed, according to the "Women, Business and the Law: Getting to Equal"[160] World Bank Group Report - from an economic perspective, investment in women and girls is a no brainer.

Take for example the cases of Malawi and Croatia, where economic investment in the empowerment of women and girls has improved the economic resilience of these countries; the global community therefore has a playbook to make progress towards increased economic security, and well-being of women and girls. Other important issues at the heart of empowerment, are the catalytic forces that will enrich society: equality and equity in the treatment of women and girls as it relates to their male counterparts. Educated girls are less likely to marry early, and more likely to practice using contraception, as stated in a report by the Bill and Melinda Gates Foundation.[161] Women who are educated and empowered economically tend to have better outcomes for their children and family; they are less likely to remain in abusive relationships, and most likely to contribute civically or economically to their communities. The children raised by these empowered women, whether male or female, tend to become members of society who carry with them the values that had been instilled in them by their mothers.

Women and girls are central to the safe and prosperous functioning of all societies across the globe.

This manifesto highlights only a small sample of some of the globe's most influential and powerful women, girls, and movements; these examples are fraught with human frailties, living in imperfect societies, but are endowed with extraordinary grit and moral conviction. In other words, we do not have to be perfect or be in the perfect context before we can make a change in the world, take a seat at the table, or create a seat for others. This manifesto attempts to cover as much as possible, including the breadth and scope of the experiences that have shaped the women featured through words and images; these are intended to capture imaginations, and shift the paradigm of societal perceptions of what women and girls are currently doing or have done, and could do globally. This manifesto aspires to inspire boys, girls, men, and women the world over - and perhaps confirm some truths and fallacies that exist in our subconscious about the resilience of women and girls - and their centrality to the survival of the human race.

Indeed, we must continue to underscore the role that women and girl intellectuals, writers, and journalists play in catalyzing peace and security, through the power of the pen and storytelling. The storyteller and historian both wield the enormous power to shape the truth, and/or tell the truth. This responsibility should not be taken lightly.

This manifesto seeks to remind its readers that all of us all citizens of the world have a social contract to leave the world that we have inherited, in a better condition than we found it; one essential part of this equation is promoting justice; justice requires equity and equality, which support bringing to bear all the elements of the local and international policies in existence in all corners of the earth. I recall the biblical story of the widows Naomi and Ruth, the story of Deborah the warrior, and Esther the Queen and how these women when given the seat at the table were able to lean in, transform their lives and the destiny of their communities towards peace and security. These biblical women left their communities better than they found them, more inclusive and perhaps even more democratic, at least for their times.

According to the National Endowment for Democracy, "…democracy involves the right of [a] people to freely determine their own destiny. The exercise of this right requires a system that guarantees freedom of expression, belief and association, free and competitive elections, respect for the inalienable rights of individuals and minorities, free communications media, and the rule of law."[162] In today's world, the concept of democracy can seem that it is just that… a concept. Sometimes democracy may embody the notion that the road to hell is paved with good intentions.

Another vantage point towards democracy is detailed in Dr. Rice's book *Democracy: Stories from the Long Road to Freedom* wherein she asserts that "only democracies have institutions that are resilient enough to protect the people's rights in the long run."[163] Underlying this assertion, is that democracy is somewhat of an experiment which provides an opportunity for citizens to decide who governs them; it is then possible that political office holders could come from across the board, that they could be inclusive of women and support their empowerment. Indeed, as political office holders often work to build upon or upend policies put into place by their predecessors, the institutions are what help to maintain a semblance of stability for the body politic. This characterization of democracy seems analogous to a marriage or, the family institution; they have different bands of characters, and are often times chaotic, messy and inconvenient but mostly nourishing. There are similar qualities that women, girls and movements display: empowering of their communities can be viewed as a stabilizing force, and create constants in a world full of destabilizing variables.

Often times, institutions, like the women, girls and movements in this manifesto, highlight the shortcomings of a society. For example, Rice cites a 2002 Arab Human Development Report, where [even with institutions] crisis may persist where there is a "freedom gap, women's empowerment gap, and/or knowledge gap…"[164] This suggests that even democracies can have gaps; especially as it relates to women's empowerment, and their peace and security. This could not have been more exemplified than in the first iterations of the U.S. Constitution. The demand for the 19th Amendment - granting women the right to vote, as well as continuous organizing towards ratification of the Equal Rights Amendment, which seeks to incorporate the equality of women - which was omitted from the due process clauses of the U.S. Constitution.

The original framers of the U.S. Constitution sought to form a more perfect union, free from the oppression of Great Britain. Unfortunately, they fell short by failing to see and acknowledge the rights and equality of half of the population. Let us also not forget the egregious violation of the rights of indigenous peoples, and enslaved Africans who were considered 3/5^{ths} of a person. This manifesto intends to spark a global discourse, and to underscore that even in the best case scenarios – e.g. the U.S. Constitutional imperative of democracy with an eye towards self-determination – these efforts can still fall short when it comes to contemplating the rights of women and other marginalized groups.

I cannot propose that there is a quick fix to these types of errors and omissions by the founders of the United States and other parts of the globe. However, I can offer a word of hope towards progress. Renewed hope towards equality, peace, and security for women and girls the world over can begin with implementing the elements of Beijing + 25, UNSCR 1325 and 1820, UN SDG 5, and other important measures highlighted in this manifesto. There are certainly others that have not been highlighted here as well that are very important. Having women at the table, letting them speak, and not appropriating their ideas is essential; acknowledging and implementing their ideas, refraining from boxing them into categories classifying who they are or who they are supposed to be is needed as well. Most importantly, acknowledging their dynamism as human beings, and harnessing this to fix the issues is paramount.

Women in leadership roles, both at grass tops and grassroots where their voices can be heard is crucial to achieving the aspirations of all the women and girls across the globe.

Finally, there remains a monumental but surmountable task before us of advancing the rights of women and girls - where there are voids or gaps in democracies as it relates to women's empowerment and equal rights –

this is coupled with the realities of failed states, conflict, strife, pandemics, violent extremism, nuclear proliferation, and broken-down institutions. The COVID-19 pandemic has highlighted the importance of fortifying our efforts to protect women and girls in the remotest parts of the world; some of whom humanitarian workers can gain access to only through numerous kilometers of travel to the most mountainous or arid parts of the world. I have been fortunate to be in the company of many of these women through my work with the World Food Programme (WFP) and on Capitol Hill. From a macro level, we need committed and sustained multilateral leadership. From a micro level, local capacity investment is critical-where we provide local women and girls resources and a seat at the table. While I was on field mission, I met a 42-year-old Syrian widowed mother of five, who through the wages she earned as a cook at WFP's school feeding program at her daughter's school was able to rally her resources to build a three room clay hut for her and her family. In that hut, she served me and other humanitarian workers delicious Syrian tea. Even in the refugee camp, she spoke to us about her dreams for her children. I vividly remember the pride with which she spoke of the academic excellence of her bright-eyed preteen daughter who attended one of the local schools facilitated in the refugee camps. Indeed, the local women leaders I met in Western Sahara walked my colleagues and I through their media and education strategy on keeping the peace and maintaining security in their communities. I departed Taiwan inspired after engaging with women serving in the Legislative Yuan, leveraging their policy agendas for the good of everyday people. Women account for 41.59 percent of lawmakers in Taiwan, the most among all the countries in Asia.[165]

The policies discussed in this manifesto are part and parcel of a body of work that continues to grow and evolve through the course of history. Hopefully, these will serve as our anchor to the ground, and as our North

Star towards protecting women and girls - not only in peace, but also in strife. This manifesto challenges simply turning a blind eye when the rights of women and girls are imperilled, whether on Wall Street, in legislatures, war-torn streets or market streets. Throughout history, the truth remains that our destinies are inextricably tied together. It is clear as day that it is beneficial to all of us to empower women and girls!

Finally, the facts suggest that we are at another precipice of a "golden hour" for gender equality, and a new global order. The question before us is what then will be our strategy and roadmap to achieve success? Whether in disease and good health, in conflict, in war, and in peace? What will success look like both globally and locally? What lessons can we draw from the women, girls and movements highlighted in the manifesto?

Part 4

A SEAT ON THEIR SHOULDERS

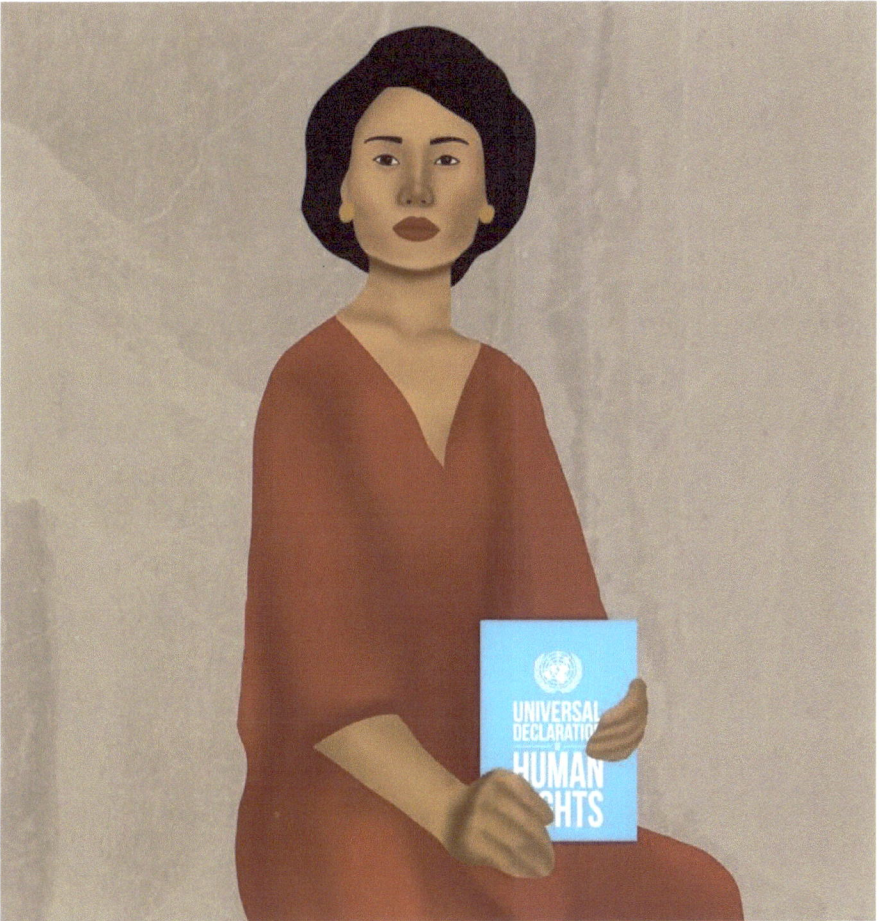

Late Sadako Ogata, Ph.D -Japanese Diplomat, Circa 1970s. Illustration by Sarah Dahir (SOUTH AFRICA)

Say Their Names and Get To Know Them

If the number of great women who I have had the great fortune of meeting in person or read about is a sign of my luck, then I am confident to say that I am quite a lucky woman. I am fortunate because I stand on their shoulders and the shoulders of my amazing fashionable 99 year old grandmother, a super smart mama, amazing aunties, and distant mommies; I stand on the shoulders of lady bosses-past and present, men, including my big brother, late papa, uncles, and male bosses who gave me books that exposed me to many other books and stories; I stand on the shoulders of the courageous women I have met in the field from Japan to Taiwan, North-eastern Nigeria, Western Sahara, Syria, Jordan and Turkey-just to name a few! I stand on the shoulders of Anne Frank and her ordeal during the holocaust, Madam Ellen Johnson Sirleaf as the first woman President in Africa and in Liberia, Benazir Bhutto as the first woman Prime Minister in Pakistan, Mary Louise McDonald as the Irish Sinn Féin's first President, and Oakland based Civil Rights Lawyer, Eva Paterson dubbed a "peaceful warrior" for fostering non-violent protest in the aftermath of the 1970 shooting of student demonstrators at Kent State University. Paterson who as a 20-year-old student leader at a time of turmoil, was catapulted into the national spotlight when she debated then President Nixon's Vice President Spiro Agnew on live television about student protests towards the impeachment of President Nixon. Vice President Agnew eventually resigned from office.[166]

True to the motif of this manifesto, Paterson met with me during the research for this book, gave me a seat at her beautiful downtown Oakland office and brought another young lawyer to the table to watch and learn! Just as she asserted in her debate with Vice President Agnew, her position was clear that non-violent protest such as during the civil rights movement were imperative towards policy change. There was also a passing of the baton approach to the manner in which Paterson approached the interview. As she was mentoring me by sharing her professional accomplishments, she included the law student so I too could mentor the law student. This nuanced experience stayed with me and continues to be something I seek to emulate. Indeed, there are a lot of great things to be said about people who are comfortable and happy to share their wealth of knowledge and pass on their legacy.

There are so many remarkable women, girls and movements to note. It was a great challenge for me to land upon which to showcase in depth in this manifesto and perhaps this means I need to have successive parts to the manifesto. Indeed, I have had the great fortune of meeting or being in the company of some of them: Deputy Secretary General Amina Mohammed, UN Women Executive Director, Phumzile Mlambo-Ngcuka, UN World Food Programme former Executive Director Ertharin Cousin, Congresswoman Sheila Jackson Lee, Speaker of the House Nancy Pelosi, Dr. Condoleezza Rice, U.S. Institute of Peace Director of Gender Policy and Strategy, Dr. Kathleen Kuehnast, and the late renowned author Toni Morrison; Morrison is one of my favourite authors, as her books *Beloved and The Bluest Eye* shook me to the core through the prose on the horrific challenges black women and girls face. Some of these distinguished women took time out of their busy schedules to sit down with me, learn about my project, and provide insights and advice. I am grateful for their trailblazing work, agency, resilience, and their commitment to helping other women and girls around the world, connecting the dots for what we can achieve together, with a seat at the table.

I see myself in every single one of these women. The final section of the manifesto is a very modest attempt to pay homage to the many women who have and continue to make an impact in the world. This is not an exhaustive list.

I would also be remiss if I failed to acknowledge the strong men who have given me wings to fly, to speak my mind, be myself and be confident. There are just way too many to mention. You all know who you are. Thank you. The success of women's empowerment, and the objectives of this manifesto can come to fruition through the full support of men and boys; they will live in a better world as a result.

Finally, this manifesto celebrates the unnamed sheroes at home, at work, from all walks of life, and in all corners of the world, who have been involved in both micro and macro movements; these sheroes have and are still making a change in peace and security, and are redrawing boundaries. Our collective actions will continue to shape the next century for women and girls. So let's make our actions count for this generation, and the many generations unborn!

Don't You Wish That You Got to Meet Them? Don't Worry, You Can Still Learn About Them

1. Upholding inclusive philosophies, legal frameworks, institutions and promoting democracy ....

    a. **The Queen**: Nzinga of Ndongo and Matamba
    b. **The Existential Philosopher:** Simone de Beauvoir
    c. **The Supreme Court Judge:** Ruth Bader Ginsburg
    d. **The Envoy:** Condoleezza Rice
    e. **The UN Under-Secretary General:** Phumzile Mlambo-Ngucka
    f. **The Governor:** Madeleine May Kunin

g. **The Speaker of the House:** Nancy Pelosi

2. Women and girls countering violent extremism ....
....

    a. **Athena:** The Goddess of Wisdom and Justice
    b. **Malala Yousafzai:** at the United Nations
    c. **Anne Frank:** at the Holocaust Memorial Museum
    d. **Alicia Garza, Patrisse Cullors and Opal Tometi:** at Black Lives Matter

3. Women leading peace processes ....

    a. **The Prophet:** Deborah of the Bible
    b. **The President:** Ellen Johnson Sirleaf
    c. **The Woman's Diplomat:** Linda Thomas Greenfield, Melanne Verveer, and Bonnie Jenkins
    d. **The Activist:** Leymah Gbowee
    e. **The Environmentalist:** Late Wangari Muta Maathai
    f. **The Economist:** Ngozi Okonjo-Iweala

4. Increasing women and girls' political leadership ....
....

    a. **The Life Pin:** Madeleine Albright
    b. **The President:** Julia Gillard
    c. **The Diplomat:** Late Sadako Ogata
    d. **The Presidential Candidate:** Hillary Clinton
    e. **The Prime Minister:** Late Benazir Bhutto
    f. **The First Lady:** Laura Bush
    g. **The Political Leader:** Stacey Abrams

    h. **The Warrior in Taiwan:** President Tsai Ing-wen

    i. **The Training Ground:** Women of Color Advancing Peace, Security and Transformation (WCAPS); Women and Girls Summit in Africa (WAGS); Leadership Council for Women in National Security (LCWINS); and ElectHER

5.   Meeting the needs of displaced women and girls …….………….. …………………………………………………………………………

    a. **The Legislators:** Nancy Pelosi, Sheila Jackson Lee, Frederica Wilson, Carolyn Maloney, Jackie Speier, and The Squad (United States Congress)

    b. **The Media:** Christiane Amanpour, Gloria Steinem, Oprah Winfrey, Amy Goodman, Aisha Seshay, Stella Paul, and Nima Elbagir

    c. **The Human Rights Lawyers:** Eva Paterson and Amal Clooney

6.   Empowering women in the military…………………………….

    a. **The Imperial Warrior:** Mulan

    b. **The United States Navy Four-star Admiral:** Michelle Howard

    c. **The Lieutenant Colonel/Legislator:** Tammy Duckworth

7.   Providing the platform for more women with disabilities…………. …………………………………………………………………………

    a. **The Poet:** Amanda Gorman

    b. **The Special Advisor for International Disabilities Right:** Judith Heumann

8. Preventing violent words and actions against women...............................
....

    a. **The Sage:** The late Maya Angelou

    b. **The Great Fire:** The late Breonna Taylor

    c. **The Survivor and Women's Rights Lawyer:** Gloria Allred

    d. **The President:** Dilma Rousseff

    e. **The Islamic Feminist:** Ayaan Hirsi Ali

    f. **The Defector:** Yeon-mi Park

    g. **The Lawyer/Diplomat:** Samantha Power

    h. **The Lawyer/Journalist:** Meghan Kelly

    i. **The Lawyer/Witness:** Anita Hill

    j. **The Member of Parliament:** The Late Jo Cox

9. Preventing sexual violence against women and girls......................
....

    a. **#Metoo**

    b. **#Timesup**

    c. **CODEPINK: Women for Peace**

    d. **HeForShe**

    e. **Let Girls Learn Initiative**

    f. **#NotTheCost: Stopping Violence Against Women in Politics**

10. Engaging male allies ....

    a. **The Spearheader:** Anwarul K. Chowdhury

    b. **The Presidents:** Joseph Biden, Barack Obama, George W. Bush and Emmanuel Macron

    c. **The Climate Czar**: John Kerry

    d. The Legislators: Male members of Legislative Caucuses on Women's Issues

    e. The Civil Society Leaders:

        i. Frederick Douglas

        ii. Bill Sweeney

        iii. Patrick Texeira and 1,000 Men Against Violence

        iv. Pravin Nikam

11. Combatting exploitation and trafficking of women and girls in conflict...

    a. The Catholic parochial, college preparatory girl's high school: Benedictine Academy

    b. The Humanitarian: Cindy McCain

    c. The NGO: Shared Hope International

    d. The Implementer: UN member states with anti-trafficking offices enforcing legislative measures and policy change

    e. Survivors

ENDNOTES

1   Lan Dong. Mulan's Legend and Legacy in China and the United States. Philadelphia: Temple University Press, 2011. Accessed February, 2021. http://www.jstor.org/stable/j.ctt14btd0g.

2   Encyclopedia Britannica, Funmilayo Ransome-Kuti | Nigerian Feminist and Political Leader. [online] Available at: https://www.britannica.com/biography/Funmilayo-Ransome-Kuti.Accessed 2020.

3   Kuti, Fela. "Unknown Solider." YouTube.com, 2016. https://www.youtube.com/watch?v=lGK_SURZCdE.

4   Johnson-Odim, Cheryl. "For Their Freedoms': The Anti-Imperialist and International Feminist Activity of Funmilayo Ransome-Kuti of Nigeria." Women's Studies International Forum 32, no. 1 (2009): 51-59. doi: https://doi.org/10.1016/j.wsif.2009.01.004.

5   Mutinda, Erick. "Remembering the Lioness of Lisabi Funmilayo Ransome Kuti – Shakarasquare," 2017. https://shakarasquare.com/remembering-the-lioness-of-lisabi-funmilayo-ransome-kuti/.

6   Kuti, "Unknown Soldier."

7   Ojewale, Oluwole. "Youth Protests for Police Reform In Nigeria: What Lies Ahead For #Endsars." Blog. Brookings Institution, 2020. https://www.brookings.edu/blog/africa-in-focus/2020/10/29/youth-protests-for-police-reform-in-nigeria-what-lies-ahead-for-endsars/.

8   "Universal Declaration of Human Rights." UN.org, 1948. https://www.un.org/en/universal-declaration-human-rights/.

9   "Image 1 of Abraham Lincoln Papers: Series 1. General Correspondence. 1833-1916: Abraham Lincoln, [March 1861] (First Inaugural Address, Final Version)," The Library of Congress, March 1861, https://www.loc.gov/resource/mal.0773800/?st=text.

10   "Women Who Shaped the Universal Declaration," United Nations. Accessed February 21, 2021, https://www.un.org/en/observances/human-rights-day/women-who-shaped-the-universal-declaration#:~:text=She%20is%20widely%20credited%20with,Universal%20Declaration%20of%20Human%20Rights.

11   "Woman Suffrage Timeline (1840-1920) — History of U.S. Woman's

Suffrage." History of U.S. Woman's Suffrage, 2020. http://www.crusadeforthevote. org/woman-suffrage-timeline-18401920.

12   Dudwick, Nora, and Kathleen Kuehnast. "Gender and Fragility: Ensuring a Golden Hour - Special Report." United States Institute of Peace, 2016. https://www. usip.org/publications/2016/11/gender-and-fragility-ensuring-golden-hour.

13   Synan, Mariel. "What is the Magna Carta?" HISTORY, 2018. https://www. history.com/news/what-is-the-magna-carta.

14   "14th Amendment Citizenship Rights, Equal Protection, Apportionment, Civil War Debt," National Constitution Center, 2021. https://constitutioncenter.org/ interactive-constitution/amendment/amendment-xiv.

15   Throughout the manifesto, the words African American, Black and persons of African descent may be used interchangeably out of respect for the non-monolithic manner in which each individual from this group identifies.

16   "Landmark Legislation: Thirteenth, Fourteenth, & Fifteenth Amendments," United States Senate, accessed February 21, 2021. https://www.senate.gov/ artandhistory/history/common/generic/CivilWarAmendments.htm.

17   Oppel, Richard A. Jr., Derrick Bryson Taylor, Nicholas Bogel-Burroughs, "What to Know About Breonna Taylor's Death," *The New York Times*, January 6, 2021, https://www.nytimes.com/article/breonna-taylor-police.html.

18   "19th Amendment to the U.S. Constitution (From the "Statutes at Large," 41 Stat. 1823)," Library of Congress, August 26, 1920, https://www.loc.gov/rr/ program/bib/ourdocs/images/41stat1823.pdf.

19   Foussianes, Chloe. "Why The Equal Rights Amendment Still Hasn't Been Adopted, Nearly a Century After It Was First Written." Town and Country, 2019. https://www.townandcountrymag.com/leisure/arts-and-culture/a32066474/equal- rights-amendment-mrs-america-era-timeline-now/.

20   Azinge, Epiphany. "The Right to Vote in Nigeria: A Critical Commentary on the Open Ballot System." Journal of African Law 38, no. 2 (1994): 173-80. Accessed 2020. http://www.jstor.org/stable/745393.

21   Mutinda, Erick. "Remembering the Lioness of Lisabi Funmilayo Ransome Kuti – Shakarasquare," 2017. https://shakarasquare.com/remembering-the-lioness-of-lis- abi-funmilayo-ransome-kuti/.

22   Hubbard, Ben. "Saudi Arabia Agrees to Let Women Drive." New York Times,

2017. https://www.nytimes.com/2017/09/26/world/middleeast/saudi-arabia-women-drive.html.

23   Attoe, Stella, and S. O Jaja. Margaret Ekpo. *Abeokuta,* Nigeria: ALF Publications, 1993.

24   National Bureau of Statistics, Nigeria. Monitoring Participation of Women In Politics In Nigeria. Abuja, Nigeria, 2016. Accessed June 15, 2020 https://unstats.un.org/unsd/gender/Finland_Oct2016/Documents/Nigeria_paper.pdf. Uglow, Jennifer S, Frances Hinton, and Maggy Hendry. The Northeastern Dictionary of Women's Biography. Boston: Northeastern University Press, 1999.

25   Chimamanda Ngozi Adichie: "I Decided to Call Myself a Happy Feminist", Minutes 0-30, Video by TEDx, 2013. https://youtu.be/hg3umXU_qWc.

26   Mutinda, "Remembering."

27   "Tynwald - Parliament of The Isle of Man - Women's Suffrage - Dates of Interest." Tynwald.Org.Im, 2020. http://www.tynwald.org.im/education/women/Pages/Dates.aspx.

28   "Women's Suffrage | Definition, History, Causes, Effects, Leaders, & Facts." Encyclopedia Britannica, 2020. https://www.britannica.com/topic/woman-suffrage.

29   Convention on the Elimination of All Forms of Discrimination Against Women." UN.org, 1979. https://www.un.org/womenwatch/daw/cedaw/.

30   Id.

31   "UNPO: Self-Determination" unpo.org, 2017. https://unpo.org/article/4957.

32   United Nations Security Council. Resolution 1325. United Nations Security Council, October 13, 2000. https://www.un.org/en/ga/search/view_doc.asp?symbol=S/RES/1325(2000).

33   "NATO/EAPC Policy for the Implementation of UNSCR 1325 on Women, Peace and Security and Related Resolutions," North Atlantic Treaty Organization, last modified August 30, 2018, https://www.nato.int/cps/en/natohq/official_texts_109830.htm?selectedLocale=en.

34   " 'How Dare You?': 16-Year-Old Greta Thunberg Thunders At UN Climate Summit," YouTube, September 23, 2019, video, 0:59, https://www.youtube.com/watch?v=M1o3NCPKZ4U.

35   National-Level Implementation, UNSCR Plans" Peace Women. Accessed 2020. https://www.peacewomen.org/member-states.

36   White House Office of the Press Secretary. Executive Order - Instituting A National Action Plan On Women, Peace, And Security, 2011. https:// obamawhitehouse.archives.gov/the-press-office/2011/12/19/executive-order-instituting-national-action-plan-women-peace-and-securit.

37   "Augustine of Hippo". En.Wikipedia.org. Accessed 2020. https://en.wikipedia.org/wiki/Augustine_of_Hippo.

38   "Justice Ruth Bader Ginsburg" Supremecourthistory.org. Accessed 2020. https://www.supremecourthistory.org/history-of-the-court/the-current-court/justice-ruth-bader-ginsburg/.

39   Ginsburg, Ruth Bader. "The Need for the Equal Rights Amendment." American Bar Association Journal 59, no. 9 (1973): 1013-019. Accessed 2020. http://www.jstor.org/stable/25726416.

40   "Historical Overview of the National Women's Party." Library of Congress. Accessed 2020. https://www.loc.gov/static/collections/women-of-protest/images/history.pdf.

41   Women Who Shaped the Universal Declaration," United Nations. Accessed 2021. https://www.un.org/en/observances/human-rights-day/women-who-shaped-the-universal-declaration#:~:text=She%20is%20widely%20credited%20with,Universal%20Declaration%20of%20Human%20Rights.

42   Ginsburg, "Equal Rights."

43   Id.

44   Id.

45   "Research Guides: American Women: Topical Essays: The Long Road to Equality: What Women Won From the ERA Ratification Effort". Guides.Loc.Gov. Accessed 2020. https://guides.loc.gov/american-women-essays/era-ratification-effort.

46   Ginsburg, "Equal Rights."

47   Id.

48   Id.

49   Id.

50   Norgren, Jill. "Belva Lockwood: Blazing The Trail for Women in Law." Prologue Magazine, 2005. https://www.archives.gov/publications/prologue/2005/spring/belva-lockwood-1.html.

51   Gates, Henry Louis Jr. "Madam Walker, The First Black American Woman to Be a Self-Made Millionaire | The African Americans: Many Rivers to Cross | PBS." The African Americans: Many Rivers to Cross. Accessed 2020. https://www.pbs.org/wnet/african-americans-many-rivers-to-cross/history/100-amazing-facts/madam-walker-the-first-black-american-woman-to-be-a-self-made-millionaire/.

52   United States v. Virginia, 518 U.S. 515 (1996).

53   Ledbetter v. Goodyear Tire & Rubber Co., 550 U.S. 618 (2007).

54   *Women, Business and The Law 2020. Washington, DC: World Bank, 2020.* https://wbl.worldbank.org/en/reports.

55   History.com Editors "Four black schoolgirls killed in Birmingham church bombing" https://www.history.com/this-day-in-history/four-black-schoolgirls-killed-in-birmingham.

56   United States Department Office of the Historian "Biographies of the Secretaries of State: Condoleezza Rice (1954–) https://history.state.gov/departmenthistory/people/rice-condoleezza.

57   "Four Black Schoolgirls Killed in Birmingham Church Bombing," History, last modified September 14, 2020, https://www.history.com/this-day-in-history/four-black-schoolgirls-killed-in-birmingham.

58   "Condoleezza Rice - People - Department of State History - Office of The Historian." History.State.Gov. Accessed 2020. https://history.state.gov/departmenthistory/people/rice-condoleezza.

59   "Functions and Powers | United Nations Security Council." UN.org. Accessed 2020. https://www.un.org/securitycouncil/content/functions-and-powers.

60   Frizzell, Neil. "How Rape Became Recognized as a War Crime." Vice.com, 2016. https://www.vice.com/enus/article/kzea53/united-nations-recognize-rape-crime-against-humanity-war-crime.

61   Lund, Georgie. "The Hidden Victims of Sexual Violence In War – World." Reliefweb. Accessed 2020. https://reliefweb.int/report/world/hidden-victims-sexual-violence-war.

62   "The Geneva Conventions and Their Commentaries." International Committee of the Red Cross, 9 July 2020. www.icrc.org/en/war-and-law/treaties-customary-law/geneva-conventions.

63   Rice, Condoleezza. *The Soviet Union and the Czechoslovak Army, 1948-1963:*

1-303, Princeton: Princeton University Press, 1984.

64   Interview with the Author and Dr. Rice, Spring 2021.

65   Rice, *"Soviet Union."*

66   Zelikow, Philip, and Condoleezza Rice. *Germany Unified and Europe Transformed.* Cambridge, Mass: 1-493 Harvard University Press, 1997.

67   Hafez, Sherine. *Women of he Midan: The Untold Stories of Egypt's Revolutionaries.* Indiana University, 2019.

68   Gbowee, Leymah, and Carol Lynn Mithers. *Mighty Be Our Powers.* HarperCollins Publisher, 2011.

69   Rice, Condoleezza. *Democracy: Stories from The Long Road to Freedom.* Grand Central Publishing, 2017.

70   "On This Day, Rosa Parks Wouldn't Give Up Her Bus Seat - National Constitution Center." Constitutioncenter.Org, 2019. https://constitutioncenter.org/blog/it-was-on-this-day-that-rosa-parks-made-history-by-riding-a-bus.

71   Rice, *"Democracy."*

72   Rice, Condoleezza. *Extraordinary, Ordinary People: A Memoir of Family.* New York: Three Rivers Press, 2011.

73   Rice, *"Extraordinary,"* 2011.

74   Dudwick and Khuenast, "Gender and Fragility."

75   Rice, *"Democracy."*

76   Vagianos, Allana. "Why Sheryl Sandberg, Condoleezza Rice and Anna Maria Chávez Want to Ban 'Bossy.'" Huffpost.com, 2014. https://www.huffpost.com/entry/ban-bossy-psa-parade_n_4906283.

77   SOCL 230 The Abject Figure: The Hottentot Venus. Minutes 0-6:49, Video by Omena Osivwemu, 2014. https://www.youtube.com/watch?v=x_qwEull3Ss.

78   Id.

79   South Africa Broadcasting Corporation News. Miss Universe Plans to Fight for Women's Rights & Against Gender-Based Violence. Minutes 0-2:18, Video, 2020. https://Youtu.Be/46Jwqjucybi.

80   The Daily Show. "Zozibini Tunzi - Becoming Miss Universe and Fighting Gender-Based Violence." Minutes 0-9:04, Video, 2019. https://www.youtube.com/watch?v=kbpm61gTJbY.

81   South Africa Broadcasting Corporation News.

82   Johnson-Sirleaf, Ellen. *This Child Will Be Great.* Harper Collins, 2009.

83   Rappler.com. "TRANSCRIPT: Miss Universe 2019 Q and A Segment." Rappler, 9 Dec. 2019, www.rappler.com/entertainment/pageants/transcript-question-and-answer-final-word-2019.

84   Id.

85   Id.

86   "Esther 4:14 New International Version," Bible Gateway, Accessed 2021. https://www.biblegateway.com/passage/?search=Esther+4%3A14&version=NIV.

87   "Malala's Story | Malala Fund." Malala.Org. Accessed 2020. https://malala.org/malalas-story.

88   Afolayan, Abiola. "Debate Item 6YL: Convention on the Rights of the Child Resolution" American Bar Association Young Lawyers Division Assembly 2014 Annual Meeting, Boston, Massachusetts.

89   "Frequently Asked Questions on the Convention on the Rights of the Child." UNICEF.Org. https://www.unicef.org/child-rights-convention/frequently-asked-questions.

90   "Let Girls Learn." USAID.gov. Accessed 2020. https://www.usaid.gov/letgirlslearn/fact-sheet.

91   Yousafzai, Malala and Christina Lamb. I *Am Malala: The Story of the Girl Who Stood up for Education and was Shot by the Taliban.* London: Weidenfeld & Nicholson, 2013.

92   "Malala Yousafzai: Nobel Peace Prize Acceptance Speech: Malala Fund Newsroom." Malala Fund | Newsroom. Accessed February 2021. https://www.malala.org/newsroom/archive/malala-nobel-speech.

93   Yousafzai and Lamb, "*I am Malala.*"

94   Dong, Lan. *Mulan's Legend and Legacy in China and the United States.* Philadelphia: Temple University Press, 2011. Accessed February 2021. http://www.jstor.org/stable/j.ctt14btd0g.

95   Id.

96   Yousafzai and Lamb, "*I am Malala.*"

97   Id.

98   Id.

99   "Greta Thunberg: Who Is She and What Does She Want?" *BBC News*, February 28, 2020. https://www.bbc.com/news/world-europe-49918719.

100 "Celebrating the Closure of CA Youth Prisons," Ella Baker Center for Human Rights. Accessed 2021, https://ellabakercenter.org/books-not-bars-victory/#:~:text=Closure%20of%20CA-,Youth%20Prisons,youth%20prisons%20will%20be%20closed.

101 "Who Was Ella Baker?" Ella Baker Center for Human Rights, Accessed 2021. https://ellabakercenter.org/who-was-ella-baker/.

102 "Nation's Premier Civil Rights Organization," NAACP, 2021. https://www.naacp.org/nations-premier-civil-rights-organization/.

103 "SCLC History" Southern Christian Leadership Conference, 2018. https://nationalsclc.org/about/history/.

104 "Ella Baker" Student Nonviolent Coordinating Committee (SNCC) Digital Gateway, Accessed 2021. https://snccdigital.org/people/ella-baker/.

105 "Lyndon B. Johnson," History, last modified November 6, 2019, https://www.history.com/topics/us-presidents/lyndon-b-johnson.

106 McCarthy, Joe. "Why Climate Change Disproportionately Affects Women." Global Citizen, 2020. https://www.globalcitizen.org/en/content/how-climate-change-affects-women/.

107 "Psalm 8." United States Conference of Catholic Bishops. Accessed February 2021. http://www.usccb.org/bible/psalms/8.

108 "Fridays for Future Is an International Climate Movement Active In Most Countries and Our Website Offers Information On Who We Are and What You Can Do." Fridays for Future. Accessed 2020. https://www.fridaysforfuture.org/.

109 "Coronavirus Disease (COVID-19) – World Health Organization." WHO.int, 2019. https://www.who.int/emergencies/diseases/novel-coronavirus-2019.

110 "Meet our Founder" About Stacey Abrams. Accessed January 20, 2021. https://fairfight.com/about-stacey-abrams/.

111 For example, Dr. Martin Luther King Jr. in America working to end racial segregation during the Civil Rights Movement, Nelson Mandela working to end apartheid in South Africa, or the current Pope Francis Jorge Mario Bergoglio

addressing the issue of sexual assault within the Catholic Church.

112 "1 Peter 2:7 New International Version" Bible Gateway, Accessed 2021. https://www.biblegateway.com/passage/?search=1%20Peter%202:7&version=NIV.

113 "Esther 4 New International Version" Bible Gateway, Accessed 2020. https://www.biblegateway.com/passage/?search=Esther+4&version=NIV.

114 "Goal 5, Gender Equality and Women's Empowerment." United Nations Sustainable Development Goals. Accessed 26 December 2020. https://www.un.org/sustainabledevelopment/gender-equality/.

115 Sample, Ian. "The Father of Climate Change." *The Guardian*, 2005. Accessed 2020. https://www.theguardian.com/environment/2005/jun/30/climatechange.climatechangeenvironment2.

116 "COP25: Thousands gather for change climate protests in Madrid." *BBC News*, December 6, 2019, https://www.bbc.com/news/world-europe-50694361.

117 Plan International. *Climate Change: Focus On Girls and Young Women*, 2020. https://plan-international.org/publications/climate-change-focus-girls-and-young-women.

118 "United Nations Framework Convention on Climate Change." United Nations, 1992. https://unfccc.int/files/essential_background/background_publications_htmlpdf/application/pdf/conveng.pdf.

119 "Climate Science Special Report Fourth National Climate Assessment (NCA4), Volume I, Executive Summary," U.S. Global Change Research Program, Accessed 2021. https://science2017.globalchange.gov/.

120 "United Nations Framework Convention on Climate Change (UNFCCC)." United Nations, 1992. https://unfccc.int/files/essential_background/background_publications_htmlpdf/application/pdf/conveng.pdf.

121 United Nations, "UNFCCC."

122 Id.

123 Bejoy Sebastian, "Five Years On, The Paris Climate Accord Needs Political Will More Than Ever," Modern Diplomacy, December 16, 2020, https://moderndiplomacy.eu/2020/12/16/five-years-on-the-paris-climate-accord-needs-political-will-more-than-ever/.

124 Thunberg, Greta. Greta Thunberg Full Speech at UN Climate Change COP25 - Climate Emergency Event. Minutes 0-11:34, Video, 2019. https://youtu.be/Eo_-

mxvGnq8.

125 Id.

126 Id.

127 Id.

128 Id.

129 "Goal 5: Achieve Gender Equality and Empower All Women and Girls," United Nations, 2021. https://unstats.un.org/sdgs/report/2017/goal-05/.

130 Natalie Robehmed, "With $20 Million Raised, Time's Up Seeks 'Equity and Safety' In The Workplace," *Forbes*, February 6, 2018, https://www.forbes.com/sites/natalierobehmed/2018/02/06/with-20-million-raised-times-up-seeks-equity-and-safety-in-the-workplace/?sh=4b9c0085103c.

131 "NWLC TIME'S UP Legal Defense Fund," National Women's Law Center (NWLC), 2021. https://nwlc.org/times-up-legal-defense-fund/.

132 "ACLU History: A Driving Force for Change: The ACLU Women's Rights Project," American Civil Liberties Union, September 1, 2010. https://www.aclu.org/other/aclu-history-driving-force-change-aclu-womens-rights-project.

133 "TIME'S UP Legal Defense Fund 'Together, We're Changing Tomorrow' 2019 Annual Report," TIME'S UP Foundation, Accessed February 21, 2021. https://timesupfoundation.org/wp-content/uploads/2020/04/2019-TULDF-Annual-Report-Final.pdf.

134 "'Silence Breakers' Behind #MeToo Movement Named Time's Person of the Year." Minutes 0-6:06, Video, 2017. https://www.youtube.com/watch?v=V3wAhkAQxZs.

135 TIME'S UP Foundation, "2019 Annual Report."

136 Id.

137 "Black Lives Matter's #What Matters 2020,"Black Lives Matter, Accessed 2021. https://blacklivesmatter.com/what-matters-2020/.

138 Gates, Henry Louis Jr., *The Signifying Monkey: A Theory of African-American Literary Criticism*, New York: Oxford University Press, 1988.

139 "The Breathe Act." Breatheact.org. Accessed 2020. https://breatheact.org/wp-content/uploads/2020/07/The-BREATHE-Act-PDF_FINAL3-1.pdf.

140 Oppel, Taylor, and Bogel-Burroughs, "Breonna Taylor's Death." *New York*

Times, September 25, 2020. https://www.nytimes.com/2020/09/25/learning/lesson-of-the-day-what-we-know-about-breonna-taylors-case-and-death.html.

141 "Black Lives Matter: What Matters 2020."Blacklivesmatter.com. Accessed 2020. https://blacklivesmatter.com/what-matters-2020/.

142 Id.

143 Black Lives Matter Global Network. "BLM on Fox." Minutes 0-3:42, Video, 2019. https://vimeo.com/373052982.

144 Id.

145 "Her Story." Black Lives Matter, Accessed February 21, 2020. https://blacklivesmatter.com/herstory.

146 Rogers, Kirsten "A Timeline of Kamala Harris' Career." IGNITE Political Power in Every Young Woman, November 7, 2020. https://ignitenational.org/blog/a-timeline-of-kamala-harris-career.

147 Id.

148 "My Story | U.S. Senator Kamala Harris of California," Harris.senate.gov, Accessed 2020. https://www.harris.senate.gov/about.

149 Holly Honderich and Samanthi Dissanayake, "Kamala Harris: The Many Identities of the First Woman Vice-President," *BBC News*, November 8, 2020. https://www.bbc.com/news/election-us-2020-53728050.

150 "My Story | U.S. Senator Kamala Harris of California." Harris.senate.gov, Accessed 2020. https://www.harris.senate.gov/about.

151 C-SPAN. "Supreme Court Nominee Brett Kavanaugh Confirmation Hearing, Day 2, Part 5." Minutes 1:13-1:45, Video, 2018. https://www.c-span.org/video/?449705-15/supreme-court-nominee-brett-kavanaugh-confirmation-hearing-day-2-part-5.

152 Burns, Alexander, and Katie Glueck. "Kamala Harris Is Biden's Choice for Vice President." New York Times, 2020. https://www.nytimes.com/2020/08/11/us/politics/kamala-harris-vp-biden.html.

153 "Beijing Declaration and Platform for Action, Beijing +25 Political Declaration and Outcome." UN Women. Accessed 2020. https://www.unwomen.org/en/digital-library/publications/2015/01/beijing-declaration.

154 Id.

155 "Goal 5, Gender Equality and Women's Empowerment." United Nations Sustainable Development Goals. Accessed 2020. https://www.un.org/ sustainabledevelopment/gender-equality/.

156 *Women, Business and The Law 2016: Getting to Equal.* Washington, DC: World Bank, 2015. https://openknowledge.worldbank.org/handle/10986/22546.

157 *Women, Business and The Law 2020.* Washington, DC: World Bank, 2020. https://openknowledge.worldbank.org/bitstream/ handle/10986/32639/9781204648153324.pdf.

158 "Women at the Table: Leymah Gbowee (Liberia) | CFR Interactives." Council On Foreign Relations. Accessed 2020. https://www.cfr.org/womens-participation-in-peace-processes/biography/leymah-gbowee-liberia.

159 Acemoglu, Daron, and James A. Robinson. *Why Nations Fail: The Origins of Power, Prosperity, and Poverty.* London: Profile Books, 2013.

160 *Women Business and the Law 2016: Getting to Equal.* Washington DC: World Bank, 2016. https://openknowledge.worldbank.org/handle/10986/22546.

161 "Bill and Melinda Gates Foundation: A Conceptual Model of Women and Girls' Empowerment." docs.gatesfoundation.org. Accessed 2020. https://docs. gatesfoundation.org/Documents/BMGF_EmpowermentModel.pdf.

162 "Founding Statement of Principles and Objectives, 1984 - National Endowment for Democracy." National Endowment for Democracy. Accessed 2020. https://www.ned.org/about/statement-of-principles-and-objectives/.

163 Rice, "Democracy."

164 Id.

165 "Taiwan has highest percentage of female lawmakers in Asia" Taiwan News: March 8, 2020. https://www.taiwannews.com.tw/en/news/3892956.

166 Eva Paterson Debating Vice President Spiro Agnew on the David Frost Show. Minutes 0-8:45, Video, 2020. https://www.youtube.com/watch?v=eje_lk6tQdg.

ABOUT THE AUTHOR

ABIOLA AFOLAYAN is an international lawyer and a member of the Bar of the Supreme Court of the United States. Her policy focus is on the humanitarian-development-peace-security nexus, human rights, the rule of law and the empowerment of women and girls.

Her portfolio includes work with the Nobel Peace Prize winning UN World Food Programme, and on Capitol Hill with field missions to the Syria/Jordan border, North-eastern Nigeria, the disputed Western Sahara region of Africa, Algeria, Turkey and Taiwan, where she saw first-hand how women were taking on leadership roles and enormous risks in telling their stories of triumph and dignity even in the eye of the storm in the context of violent extremism and all manner of atrocities that threatened their livelihoods.

Abiola was also guest lecturer at Temple University School of Law International Law Program in Rome, Italy where she has discussed UN Security Council Resolution 1325 on Women, Peace and Security.

She is former foreign affairs staffer for a senior member of the U.S. Congress who is the first woman Ranking Member on the House Judiciary Subcommittee on Crime, Terrorism, Homeland Security, and Investigations. Upon the request of the Member, Abiola worked on legislative measures and initiatives on women, peace and security, including a Capitol Hill Congressional Briefing Series which earned the Member of Congress the Charles T. Manatt Democracy Award, in Washington, DC.

She has been an active member of the American Bar Association (ABA) with appointments and service in various capacities: Young Lawyers Division Scholar, Chairwoman of the Young Lawyers Division International Committee, Council Member of the Rule of Law Initiative for Africa, ABA Presidential Appointee to the Center for Children and the Law and Taskforce for Unaccompanied Minors, and with the Section of Environment, Energy, and Resources-Congressional Relations Committee.

As the founder of Not On Our Watch Advocacy! (NOOWA!), an anti youth trafficking NGO, she partnered with the New Jersey Attorney General's office and the ABA Task Force on Human Trafficking on public awareness initiatives.

Within the ABA, she co-authored various measures, including resolutions that passed in the Young Lawyers Division General Assembly on the due process rights of unaccompanied minors and the Convention on the Rights of the Child (CRC).

Abiola is active in various organizations: Most Influential Persons of African Descent (MIPAD), Women of Color Advancing Peace Security and Conflict Transformation (WCAPS), as a National Endowment for Democracy Penn Kemble Democracy Forum Fellow, Center for Strategic and International Studies (CSIS) Africa Policy Accelerator and Partnership for a Secure America cohort member, and advisory committee member for the Women and Girls Africa Summit (WAGS) Friends of Africa.

She can be reached at:

Email: abiolaafolayan@gmail.com

Instagram: abiola_afolayan_1325

Twitter: @abiolaoafolayan

www.ingramcontent.com/pod-product-compliance
Lightning Source LLC
Chambersburg PA
CBHW040823300326
41914CB00063B/1482